How to Become a

Successful

Black Man

The Men Tell Their Story

HILLARY DRUMMOND SIMPSON

Text Copyright © 2012 Hillary Drummond Simpson

All rights reserved. No part of this book may be reproduced, stored in a retrieval system, or transmitted by any means without the written permission of the author.

Requests for permission to make copies of any part of the book should be emailed to: shsimpo@aol.com

ISBN-13: 978-1534961531

ISBN-10: 1534961534

Printed in the U. S. A.
First Printing, September 2012

Because of the dynamic nature of the Internet, any web addresses or links contained in this book may have changed since publication and may no longer be valid. The views expressed in this work are solely those of the author and do not necessarily reflect the views of the publisher, and the publisher hereby disclaims any responsibility for them.

Dedication

To my children—Suzette, Gavin and Dana

Grandson- Jonah

All African American Boys

Gavin Simpson

Table of Contents

Acknowledgments ix

Destined for College—Or So I Thought! 1

Trials of My Own Son 6

Boys in Crisis 15

Where Are All Our Black Men? 20
    President Barack Obama President of the United
        States of America 31

Successful Men in the Arts 36
    Lance Darden Computer Animator 36
    Omar Rashad Tyree New York Times Best-Selling
        Author and Speaker 42

Successful Men in Healthcare 51
Michael L. Penn Jr. M.D.; Ph.D. Scientist/Physician 51
    Dr. Daryl Sherrod Internist 57
    Aaron Scott Chief Nuclear Technologist 62

    Marcus Fields Registered Nurse Nurse of the Year
        2009 67

Successful Men in Education 74
    Dr. Samuel Taylor King School Superintendent. 74
    Chike Akua Educational Consultant, Speaker,
        Author..78
    Dorrian Randolph Teacher 82
    Dr. Stephen Appea School Principal 90

Successful Men in Business... 98
    Hezekiah Griggs III Entrepreneur, President, and
        CEO, HG3 98
    Richard B. Jefferson, Esq. Entertainment Attorney,
        M.E.T.A.L. Law Group, LLP....................................102
    Maurice Hurst Electrical Engineer 108
    *W. Anthony Drummond Entrepreneur, Certified
        Public Accountant, Hotel Owner, Author...........115

How Important Should Sports Be in Your Son's Life?.............. 119
    Julani Ghana Sports Manager.......................................119

What I Learned and You Can Too.......................................138

A Few Words for the Boys..153

Be Smart in Dealing with the Law 157

References 162

Acknowledgments

First, I would like to thank my son for inspiring the conception of this book. Even though at times motherhood has been challenging, I would have never experienced the difficulties an African American boy goes through to become an adult if I was not a mother to one. This experience has helped me to see not only their tremendous talent and potential, but also their struggles, insecurities and the tremendous role their social environment plays on their lives... I wish him only the best and know that one day, with hard work, his dream will be realized.

Thanks also to all the boys that I have taught at Dr. Rose B. English School in Brooklyn, New York, Cleveland School in Newark, New Jersey and Sims Elementary School in Conyers, Georgia. You have given me a wealth of knowledge and I hope you will all realize your potential and become successful men. To the boys that have joined the "Boys to Men" program which I created at Cleveland and Sims schools, I hope you have been helped by having a deeper relationship with the men in your lives. I also hope the dads, uncles and big brothers understood the importance of being a positive role model in the lives of a young boy.

A very, very special thanks to my Aunt Merlyn for her precise work in editing and her invaluable advice on the book's content.

Special thanks to my family for their encouragement and support.

I am sorry that my dad did not live to see this book published but he has inspired me as the first successful black man I know. He has been included as the last of the successful men in this book. Much of the interview was done before he passed away in January, 2009. His strength, courage, drive and tremendous ambition has energized and made me extremely proud.

Chapter 1

Destined for College—Or So I Thought!

"Mom, I am not going to college; it's not for me!" These words pierced my brain like the screech of a tire before a car crash. I felt like my circulation was being cut off. My son blurted this at me during a parent-teacher conference with his math teacher. He was seventeen years old and one year away from high school graduation. The words seemed unreal; there was never a thought that he would not go to college. In my mind, my son was going to be great! He would attend the college where most famous black men went, because he would become one of them. He would attend the prestigious Morehouse College in Atlanta. My dad graduated from college in England and my brother graduated from Harvard University. I couldn't wait to see who my son would become. After all, in my family, men are a rarity, and I was proud to have a son.

Maybe my son felt that in front of the math teacher was the safest place to deliver this news; he could share it without having to witness my deep disappointment alone. Nevertheless, I cried for days, hoping he would change his mind. Weeks later, when I was able to approach

the subject with him again, he informed me that his gifts were not academic but musical, and he did not need a college education to be successful. He summed it up rather politely when he said, "Those were your dreams for me, not my dreams for me." I could not argue with him because he was correct. I appreciated how he put it into perspective for me but I still wish that our dreams were the same.

Though I respected his self-analysis, I could not so easily give up on my dream of college for him so I explained how a college education could help his music career; when that method of reasoning failed, I pleaded with him to put plans B and C in place by choosing alternate careers in case the music did not work. It was no use; he argued that he needed to put all his energies into his music to ensure success. Reluctantly, I agreed but insisted on high school graduation and doing positive music that could uplift others. He did graduate and was proud of himself. So was I. But this wasn't the path I had envisioned for him.

First, let's define *success*. If you ask one hundred people this question, you would get one hundred different answers but for the purpose of this book, I would like to narrow this down to a working definition. In my opinion, a man is successful if he sets and achieves his career goals which help him to financially support himself and his family. Others would define him as successful if he makes a six-figure income, lives in a big house, and drives a nice car. As a mom and an educator, I believe that college is an important road to success. I am not saying that you have to go to college to be successful because our world is full of successful people who have not gone to college. But living in the twenty first century has become so competitive that a college education is frequently a prerequisite to show your skills. Having a good education also gives a sense of confidence that helps you navigate your way through life easier. Statistics show that people with a college degree earn more than those without. However, I found raising my son to see college as the next logical phase after high school difficult. I am sure his gift of music had a lot to do with it, because he kept telling me that school was not as easy for him as it was for me. As an educator, I understood that well. But according to the experts, we shouldn't have a problem. According to them, if kids come from a household in which the parents and grandparents have gone to college, they will see college in their future. After all, we were a middle-class, two-parent household; I am college educated with two master's degrees, and also graduated from the New York University (NYU) School of Business. His father was not college educated but was very hard working. My mom and dad are college educated, and my older daughter graduated from NYU Law School. But having all these credentials and connections was no insurance that my son would go to college. Reconciling that has been extremely difficult for me.

Why do so many of our boys underachieve in school and not see college in their future? Is it because of the lack of role models? Is it how we rear them or a combination of both? I see too many moms who love their sons but do not give them enough responsibility. In hindsight, I think I have been guilty of this. I see too many others who do not give them enough attention and turn them out too early because they made a mistake. We do not make them accountable enough and do not challenge them enough. I believe that part of the problem is that our expectations are too low. We usually compare our kids to others in the neighborhood and feel ok since he is not involved in anything illegal (that we know of) or that he may not be in jail. We cannot continue to produce men who are unprepared to become effective fathers and husbands. Yes, racism still prevails, but we must stop blaming others for this cycle and take full responsibility. Maybe then, we will see changes. It is not easy, but if we seek, we can find a way. No one else will solve our problems, we have to roll up our sleeves and tackle them ourselves.

I cannot help but feel somewhat responsible for my son's current lack of college preparedness, even though all he wants to do is music. How did this happen? What should I have done differently? Or is it as my son explained, "Going to college is your plan for me, it is not my plan for me." How do other families rear their black sons and make them academically successful? Are the most successful ones academically gifted? Is it nature, nurture, or is it a combination of the two? How do you save a black son from a negative environment when he does not feel like he is academically gifted? How do you as a mom make him into the man he needs to be especially if his dad is not actively involved in his life? Can you love and protect your son too much and disable him? I had all these questions, and I needed them answered for myself and other mothers.

Chapter 2

Trials of My Own Son

What My Husband and I Tried to Do "Right"

I was 26 years old, married and still attending college full time at the birth of my son. I was a marketing and management major attending New York University and also working part-time. My husband would do most of the rearing since he came home in the early afternoon. He was a chef who worked the early shift. We were very happy with our babysitting arrangement. You see, my son was special, and we needed someone to give him all the attention and love he would need. The babysitter was Haitian and poor but showed great respect for her family. When her kids went to school, my son was her pride and joy, and that was the way we wanted it. Even though I could not be home days, my son would be raised by a "loving and doting mom." He had a great childhood! He started preschool at three and was effervescent, funny and loved to eat. His preschool teacher once wrote, "He debates like a lawyer and frequently cleans his plate at lunch." My son has a great voice and became a part of the elementary school chorus. They would sing at the *Daily News* Building in New York City on holidays and perform in the school auditorium.

At age eight, after singing a duet with his friend Juan in private school, he decided he would become a singer. Of course I was excited for him. I did not know where he'd gotten the voice, since neither my husband nor I have such gifts. Nevertheless, we loved to hear him sing. Between the ages of fourteen and fifteen, however, he gave me the shock of my life. He decided he wanted to be a "rapper"! How could my son want to be a rapper? I did not enjoy rap music. I didn't even play it in my house since it seemed like the artists celebrated violence and denigrated women. This was back in the late nineties when rap was extremely popular. After careful consideration, and learning a little about teen psychology, I decided not to fight it but be supportive. However, I told him that his music needed to be positive. I dismissed it hoping it would wear off, since most black boys at that time either wanted to be rappers or play for the NFL or NBA.

We sent him to private school between kindergarten and second grade, because we wanted the best for him, and if it meant making a sacrifice, then we were willing to do that. Only later did I realize that the teaching was not excellent and the kids would behave disrespectfully in the classroom without much supervision. After a year or two, we pulled him out. I had mixed feelings about having him in the same school with me, but he completed his elementary education in the public school where I taught. For middle school, we put him back in private school, but unfortunately the school closed down after a year, so he went back to public school for a few months.

We moved from Brooklyn, New York, to one of the top school districts in New Jersey in the winter of 1995, my son was twelve years old. You see, I did not want my son growing up in an urban area with its propensity to destroy black boys. I felt I had two choices: either he could grow up in a mostly white community and be judged negatively because of his race and skin color or my greatest fear—he might not live to grow up at all if he continued to live in the city. At the time, there were so many drive-by shootings on the news, and many of the casualties were innocent bystanders. Additionally, my neighbors' children, in particular the boys, were constantly being taken in to the police station because a group of them gathered outside talking. This was in the early nineties. It was called "loitering." Although the community we lived in Brooklyn was considered a "middle-class neighborhood", black boys were still in danger of being locked up because they were standing together on the street talking. (There was no front or back yards.)

I could not stand by and see my child become the victim of prejudice and violence, so I convinced my husband that we should move to a school district where the school system was highly rated and where people were middle class and educated. I had read somewhere that white folks who were more educated were less prejudiced. I spent a long time doing the research and came up with the ideal town in suburban New Jersey.

We bought a lovely home with a park-like backyard and a huge swimming pool. The downside was that my husband and I both had to drive fifty miles each way to work daily. My husband left at 3:00 a.m. and was back home by 1:00 p.m. I carpooled and was home by 5:00 or 6:00 p.m. Commuting was terrible, but I loved the suburbs and I felt it was the price I had to pay for safety for my children.

My Son's Education—both in and out of School

Living in a middle-class, white suburb has its advantages and disadvantages. We felt physically safe, and my children also loved our home, but they had quite an adjustment. Although my daughter was the only black in almost all of her classes from first through fifth grade, she had lots of friends. My son, however, had a hard time adjusting, as he started feeling the prejudice immediately.

When he went in the supermarket, for example, he said he felt awful when old white ladies would clutch their bags closer upon seeing him. My heart sank, and I silently cried. He was accused the second day after moving in the neighborhood of stealing a bike, simply because we lived close to a 7-Eleven. Later, the kids in the neighborhood found out that one of their friends had taken it as a prank. In both instances, my heart sank deeply into the pit of my stomach, and I wondered if I had made the right decision. I knew it was not going to be easy, but I would rather see my son alive facing prejudice than having him killed on the street by some senseless drive-by shooting.

Social Strain on the Street

I decided to immerse myself in forming an African-American cultural association to serve as a resource for the 2 percent of African-American parents and kids who were living in the township. The community was very diverse, with sixty-seven different languages spoken in the high school, and the Chinese and Indian populations had their own formal organizations. Our group grew and became known in the community as a resource to the township and its African-American residents. I actually loved living in my new community.

But nothing was able to shelter my son from being treated as a black man living in a white suburb. He was tall, muscular, bald, and dark-skinned. As soon as he started driving, he was pulled over for the silliest of reasons. One of the more strange events was when he was stopped on his block while jogging and asked to show his ID. This was 8.00 a.m. Immediately, two backup police cars came and said they had received a phone call that a black man was on the block sitting in a van. My son was properly interrogated about his reason for jogging without an ID and then was allowed to go home. It is important to note that he had lived on that small block since he was twelve. He was twenty by then and was clearly a threat, being a full-grown black man. As a mom, I feared for my son's safety, and my husband and I kept explaining how he should act if pulled over.

Frustration at the obvious racism in the system tugged at his heart strings, and we kept encouraging him to work with it and do nothing out of place. My son didn't drive a nice car, but he was given tickets for stopping over the white line, having an air freshener hanging from his rearview mirror, dropping off a passenger in front of his house instead of pulling in the driveway at midnight, and sitting in his car parked in front of his house instead of pulling in the driveway.

One night, he was sitting in front of the house with his best friend, and the cops came for a second time asking for his ID. He explained that he lived there and was tired of having to prove his address. They insisted he show proof, so he told them he was going inside to prove it. Obviously, the two cops were very upset when he went inside and never returned. They gave his friend a ticket for parking illegally. A few days later, the same cops (my son had described them) came to my house at about four in the morning saying there was a call that someone had fallen. I explained to them that we did not call and we were sleeping. They then asked if anyone else lived there. We told them that our son did but was not home. They asked for us to check to be sure. When we went inside, the two cops came in after us uninvited to see if my son was home. We later found out that these were the same two officers who had wanted my son to show ID before. Why did they obviously lie to come into my house at 4:00 a.m.? To prove to my son their power and that if they wanted him, they could get him?

There were many other incidents, but one in particular when my son called to say he was outside and cops were there asking him for his ID *again*. He said he did not want to come out of the car again since we warned him to make no sudden movements. It was about midnight, and my usually quiet husband ran out and yelled, "Leave him alone; he can't take anymore!" Of course I ran behind him to explain to the officers that this was a constant problem. I asked why it was a crime to sit in your car with your girlfriend in front of your house. They claimed there had been a "rash of robberies in the area" and they had to check. It ended amicably when they realized that I worked with the mayor's office, knew the police chief, had my own cable TV show, and was very active in the township. However, the harassment did not stop there.

A few weeks later, he was pulled over for stopping over the white line. He was told to get out of the car, which he did. They then handcuffed him and said they were going to search the car while his girlfriend and cousin were still sitting there. Immediately, one of the officers pulled out a little clear bag and said, "Look what we found!" My son told him that he did not find that in his car, and he must have put it there. They had my son sit in the back of the cop car while they manhandled his girlfriend and were rude and disrespectful to them. All the time, they were in the car, they were laughing. They then let my son out of the handcuffs and gave him a few tickets. That was enough! We could take no more.

I made a formal complaint to the Human Relations Council, who then requested a meeting with the township police and the mayor's office. In attendance were members of the Human Relations Council, the mayor, the police chief, my son, his girlfriend, her parents, my friend who was an attorney and the mayor of the adjoining town, my husband, and me. We talked about him being harassed by township officers, and they talked about him cooperating with police when stopped. My husband also complained about being stopped many mornings at 3:00 a.m. going to work. My family, the members of the council, and my friend expressed concern about the fact that they were wearing down my son's confidence as a man and also violating his civil rights.

The meeting seemed to be productive, and we were encouraged to file a complaint with the police department. We did, but that was obviously a big mistake! A few days later, my cell phone rang at 3:00 a.m., and when I picked it up, it registered the complaint department of the police station. No one answered when I picked up, but every morning after that, my phone would ring at the same time, but there would be no registered number. The number had been blocked. But sure enough, that call came in at the same time *every morning for one full year!* No one could trace the call—not even the phone company. I had to make sure to turn my phone off every night. Sure enough, the next day, my phone would show that I had missed a call at 3:00 a.m. We were harassed for making that complaint and asking for the tape to be reviewed the night they put my son in handcuffs. Obviously, if my son had had drugs in the car, they would have arrested him. But he was released. If we had not had great connections in town, my son would have been put away a long time ago, just for being black and visible.

Chapter 3

Boys in Crisis

Having been an educator for over twenty years and working in different states, I find that most African-American boys aspire to be rappers or NFL/NBA stars. They are hard pressed to find another career. You may find a few who choose to be firemen or corrections officers since they are familiar with those careers. But overwhelmingly, they choose entertainment or sports. Even when they hear about the odds of ever playing on a team or becoming a famous rapper, they still say that is their dream. I would always tell them about the pros and cons of these careers and ask them to write about a backup career in case they don't make it as a rapper or a professional player. That is when their pencils get frozen on the page ... they have difficulty finding another career.

Could it be that those are the jobs they see as possible for African-

American men? Are these the roles in which they see African American men excel on TV? What if we exposed them to the different influential careers black men have and tell them how they succeeded? Maybe then they could see themselves in those careers as well.

For this book, I decided to go to the source: *successful black men.* I needed to find out how they were reared, how they handled the challenges in life, and what advice they would give parents today in developing successful black men. In all cases, they were also asked to give advice directly to the boys. In one case, we also hear from a mom; in another, we hear from a manager of professional athletes where he reveals to parents and children the facts about a career as a professional player. This I believe will give our boys a more balanced and realistic assessment of a career that seems so glorified. Maybe, our parents and boys will see a whole new world that is accessible to them.

It is time for change! If Barack Obama can become the first African-American president of the United States, black boys and black men can change their image. *Yes, we can ... because we have no choice ... We must!*

Let's take the blinders off for a moment and look at our current situation.

Boys score lower than girls on standardized tests

According to the National Center for Education Statistics 2000, "Boys in elementary through high school score significantly lower than girls on standardized measures of reading, and they are 5 times more likely to undergo learning or disabilities placement."

In 2008, the statistics were no better.

- Boys are 30 percent more likely than girls to flunk or drop out of school.

- When it comes to grades and homework, girls outperform boys in elementary, secondary, high school, college, and even graduate school.

- Boys are four to five times more likely than girls to be diagnosed with Attention Deficit Hyperactivity Disorder (ADHD).

- Women outnumber men in higher education with 56 percent of bachelor's degrees and 55 percent of graduate degrees going to women.

- Boys make up two-thirds of the students in special education.

When it comes to the African-American male children, the statistics are even worse!

- According to a 2006 report from the Schlott Foundation, 58 percent of black boys do not graduate from high school and in New York City only 26 percent do.

- Seventy percent of black children are growing up in single-parent households (the majority without a father figure).

- Forty percent of African-American women between the ages of 18 and 24 attended college while only 25 percent of the men in that age group attended.

- In 1996, only 35 percent of those men graduated within six years from NCAA Division I schools.

So if we start with one hundred men, twenty-five will attend college and only eight will end up graduating in six years. *A loss of over 90 percent of our men! Incredible!*

In 2010, fourteen years later, the American Council on Education (ACE) released its annual status report on minorities in higher education. The report showed that the proportion of black men attending college had risen to 37 percent, while for black women it had risen to 42 percent. The most disturbing part is that the graduation rate remained the same for black men, while the female graduation rate jumped to 45 percent, leaving some college campuses with twice as many black female graduates as black male graduates.

- *The graduation rate for black men is the lowest of any*

population (American Council on Education).

According to Jawanza Kunjufu, famed writer of African-American books, "African Americans are the only group in America in which females outnumber males (800,000 to 500,000) in college enrollment.

So then we see that our black men are not graduating from college . . .

Where then are our black men?

Chapter 4

Where Are All Our Black Men?

Looking for Black Men

It seems like everyone is looking for the black male. Black women are looking for a good black man to marry; black children are looking for the black male to mentor and guide them; the schools are looking for black male teachers to inspire and serve as role models; pastors are looking for the black male to serve as deacons; and our colleges are looking for more black male graduates.

Here is the sad truth . . .

Black men have higher incarceration rates than any other group

A study done by the Justice Policy Institute finds that the number of black men in jail or prison has increased five times higher than twenty years ago.

A *New York Times* article from 2008 commented on

this trend:

> "The number of black men in jail or prison has grown fivefold in the past 20 years, to the point where more black men are behind bars than are enrolled in colleges or universities. The increase in the black male prison population coincides with the low college enrollment rate of AA young men". (*New York Times*, Nov. 20, 2008)

If we were to look at the raw census data from the Bureau of Justice, we would see that *more black men are incarcerated than any other group.*

As of June 30, 2007, the incarceration rate for men in state, federal, or county jail was 1,406 per 100,000 residents. However the rate for white males is only 773 per 100,000, while the rate for black males is 4,618 per 100,000—nearly seven times the incarceration rate of the white male. *Source: Bureau of Justice Policy Report*

More black men are serving time for drug offenses than any other group.

Of the 253,300 prison inmates serving time for drug offenses at the end of 2005, 20 percent were white, 28 percent were Hispanic, and a whopping 45 percent were black!

Nationwide, black men are sent to prison on drug charges at

thirteen times the rate of white men, but according to the same census, "most drug offenders are white. Five times as many whites use drugs as blacks. Yet blacks comprise the great majority of drug offenders sent to prison . . ."

According to the federal Household Survey, "most current illicit drug users are white. There were an estimated 9.9 million whites (72 percent of all users), 2.0 million blacks (15 percent), and 1.4 million Hispanics (10 percent) who were current illicit drug users in 1998," And yet, blacks constitute 36.8 percent of those arrested for drug violations, over 42 percent of those in federal prisons for drug violations. African Americans comprise almost 58 percent of those in state prisons for drug felonies; Hispanics account for 20.7 percent."

Source: Substance Abuse and Mental Health Services Administration, National Household Survey on Drug Abuse: Summary Report 1998 (Rockville, MD: Substance Abuse and Mental Health Services Administration, 1999)

Blacks are more likely to be sent to prison for drug offenses

Among persons convicted of drug felonies in state courts, whites were less likely than African Americans to be sent to prison. Thirty three percent (33%) of convicted white defendants received a prison sentence, while fifty one percent (51%) of African-American defendants received prison sentences.

Source: Durose, Matthew R., and Langan, Patrick A., Bureau of Justice Statistics, *State Court Sentencing of Convicted Felons, 1998 Statistical Tables* (Washington DC: US Department of Justice, December 2001) Table 25

Black men are more likely to be sent to prison for any offense than any other group

In 2001, the chances of going to prison were highest among black males (32.2%) and Hispanic males 17.2% and lowest among white males (5.9%) The lifetime chances of going to prison among black females 5.6% were nearly as high as for white females. Hispanic females (2.2%) and white females 0.9% had much lower chances of going to prison

More black men are incarcerated for custody cases than any other group.

Black males ages thirty to thirty-four had the highest custody (child support) incarceration rates of any race, gender, or group at mid-year 2007.

Black males represent the largest percentage of inmates held in custody (35 percent), compared to other races: white males (32 percent) and Hispanic males (17 percent

(*Source*:www.hrw.org/campaigns/drugs/war/keyfacts.htm)

More black men die with AIDS-related illnesses than any other group.

"... Of the forty-two inmates who died from AIDS-related illnesses in 2000, thirty-eight were male and four were female. Those who died from Aids-related illnesses were most likely black. Over the three year period beginning in 2000, a total of 155 local jail inmates died from Aids-related causes."

(*Source*:www.ojp.usdoj.gov/bjs/pub/pdf/hivpjo2.pdf)

Source: Bonczar, Thomas P., US Department of Justice, Bureau of Justice Statistics, Prevalence of Imprisonment in the US Population 1974-2001

Many Black Men spend their prime years under Correctional Supervision

One in three black men between the ages 20 and 29 years old is under correctional supervision or control.

Source: Mauer, M. & Huling, T., Young Black Americans and the Criminal Justice System: Five Years Later (Washington DC: The Sentencing Project, 1995)

More Black Men are disenfranchised than any other group

"Thirteen percent of all adult black men—1.4 million—are disenfran-chised, representing one—third of the total disenfranchised population and reflecting a rate of disenfranchisement that is seven times the national average. Election voting statistics offer an approximation of the political importance of black disenfranchisement: 1.4 million black men are disenfranchised compared to 4.6 million black men who voted in 1996."

Source: Fellner, Jamie and Mauer, Marc, "Losing the Vote: Impact of Felony Disenfrachisement Laws in the United states" (Washington DC: Human Rights Watch & The Sentencing Project, 1998) p.8

When we consider the US Census Bureau Statistics 2000, whites account for 69 percent of the US population, blacks 12.1 percent, Hispanics 12.5 percent, Asians 3.8 percent, and Native Americans 0.7 percent. This would mean that out of every 10 people, 7 would be white and 1.2 would be black. Now compare this to the incarceration rate: *the black male is incarcerated at nearly seven times the rate of the white male.* In June 2009, the rate of black to white imprisonment held about the same rate, with black men being incarcerated at a rate of 4,749 per 100,000 residents while white males were at only 708 inmates per 100,000 residents.

Now we see why 70 percent of black children are growing up in single-parent households. Now we see why black women are having a difficult time finding black men to marry. Now we see why black male mentors are difficult to come by. Our black men are incarcerated in unimaginable numbers! It should be a national crisis.!!!

"The racially disproportionate nature of the war on drugs is not just devastating to black Americans. It contradicts faith in the principles of justice and equal protection of the laws that should be the bedrock of any constitutional democracy; it exposes and deepens the racial fault lines that continue to weaken the country and belies its promise as a land of equal opportunity; and it undermines faith among all races in the fairness and efficacy of the criminal justice system. Urgent action is needed, at both the state and federal level, to address this crisis for the American Nation."

www.hrw.org/campaigns/drugs/war/keyreco.htm

Source: *Rights Key Recommendations from Punishment and Prejudice: Racial Disparities in the War on Drugs (Washington, DC: Human Watch, June 2000*

"Our criminal laws, while facially neutral, are enforced in a manner that is massively and pervasively biased. The injustices of the criminal justice system threaten to render irrelevant fifty years of hard fought civil rights progress."

Source: Welch, Ronald H. and Angulo, Carlos T., *Justice on Trial: racial Disparities in the American Criminal Justice System* (Washington, DC: Leadership Conference on Civil Rights/Leadership Conference Education Fund, May 2000)

Flawed System

Clearly, the system is flawed and needs to be corrected. We see that black men in prison has become as American as apple pie. There is no outcry about this. It seems to me that this should cause a state of emergency. After all, this does not just affect the black community, it affects all of America. Black people are part of the American fabric. America is regarded as the richest and most respected country in the world and what does this say about our system of justice? Is everyone being treated fairly under the law? But more importantly, is incarceration rehabilitating these men? Is that the most effective way to spend our tax dollars? How do these men fit back into society when they are released? How does this affect the black family, community and therefore our country? And as an African American woman, I want to know if these men are all locked away and do not go to college, who is going to anchor strong families in the community? Who will the young boys emulate as they grow into young men? In my opinion, the money should be spent on education and rehabilitation so that these men can reenter society.

Spending the money on treatment programs may be a more effective alternative to reduce recidivism. But this book is not about blame. We have Reverend Al Sharpton and other civil rights leaders fighting our cause, and more of us need to join them because it is obvious that there is a lot of work to be done. But in this book, which is intended for the black family, we will take responsibility for our own failures. Only then can we seek to find a solution. Blaming others will not help us find solutions. There are a lot of reasons for these troubling statistics, but the fact is almost all jobs require high school or college—hence, I believe one of the biggest problem—lack of academic preparation. Another problem is our culturally reinforced stereotypes of what a black male is supposed to be. Statistics show that we spend more hours watching TV than reading books or having a discussion. So much of what our boys learn is from TV role models.

The truth is black boys will become who we teach them to be and the question is who is that? They are bombarded with the image of a black male as having athletic prowess, criminal deviance, or drug dealer turned rapper turned millionaire. Do these images and the music they listen to have an effect on who they become?

How This Book Can Help

Raising children is not easy, we tend to raise our children the way we were raised. It may have worked for our parents' generation, but our children today are growing up in a much different world than we did. Take for example the work that is expected of a fourth-grader today. I learned much of that stuff in high school! Children are expected to know more much earlier. Today, children are growing up with advanced technology like computers, iPods, iPads, texting, sexting and with that comes social media like facebook and twitter. A child can find constant entertainment with the touch of a button. But schooling requires focus, concentration, and discipline. Learning becomes more difficult if the parent does not monitor and help them manage these outside influences.

How can we, as parents, raise the next generation of black boys to respect education and to be more disciplined and diligent? How can we teach them that hard work helps them to develop self-discipline and self-respect? How can we teach them to delay gratification so that their lives can be more full, rich, and meaningful? How can we raise our boys so that they can play an active role in the world and become contributing citizens of society? How can we teach them what it takes to be a man?

We know this can happen because despite the odds, there are many successful African-American men. Maybe we need to find out how they did it and emulate them. I decided to study successful men to find out how they made it, while so many others didn't. These men don't just have great jobs; they are also men of great character. See how they grew up, how they conquered peer pressure, and what advice they have for parents raising African-American boys today.

PRESIDENT BARACK OBAMA

President of the United States of America

First Black President of the United States

At this time in American history, we have been graced with an African-American president. It would be irresponsible not to give honorable mention to the most recognized face of African-American male success: President Barack Obama. Although he was not available for an interview, President Obama relayed his wishes for success for this book through the press department of the White House.

The president's life growing up is well documented in his autobiography *Dreams from My Father*. So I thought it would be a good idea to review his life. Like 70 percent of African-American children today, he did not grow up with his father. However, President Obama had much support during his childhood, which contributed to his success today.

Loving and Supportive Family

Young Barack was blessed to have a loving, supportive mother and grandparents. His grandfather, Stanley Dunham, lovingly called "Gramps," was very adventurous and enjoyed regaling his grandson with grand stories about the boy's father. He told his grandson that one thing he could learn from his dad, Barack Obama Sr., was confidence.

Male Guidance

When Barack and his mother moved to Indonesia to live with her new husband, Lolo, he made sure Barack (Barry) was treated as his own son. At one point, when it seemed that young Barry would become a victim of neighborhood bullies, his stepfather gave him hours of boxing lessons and taught him the importance of being prepared. When asked about the most important skill he needed as a man, his stepdad responded quickly, "Strength, if you can't be strong, be clever."

Committed Mother

Stanley Anna Dunham, his mother (named Stanley because her father wanted a boy), no doubt loved and was committed to her son. When he received a cut on his arm from mud-sliding with his friend, his mom naturally became frantic. Her husband tried to convince her to wait until the following day, but she practically browbeat her neighbor into driving them to the hospital immediately. Being a single mom, she never allowed Barack's absence to be an excuse for him to slack off or not always do his best. She realized that his only chance to become successful was to get a good education, so she would wake him every morning at 4:00 a.m. five days a week for three hours of English study! When he complained, she responded, "This is no picnic for me either, Buster." His complaints did not deter her. She knew what she needed to do as his mom, and she was committed to him getting the best education. As a white mother to a black child, she exposed him to his history and taught him lessons of honesty, fairness, straight talk, and independent judgment. She could have easily taught her son to dislike his father, but she filled his head with positive things about Barack Sr. Even though his mother was equally intelligent, she explained his thick eyebrows by saying, "Your eyebrows are from me, but your brains are from your father."

So even though Barack did not grow up with his father, he did not use that as an excuse to live a mediocre life. Of course, he later had to reconcile his absence in his life. But he used his lack of a father to fuel the fire to be the committed father he is today. More important, he was able to identify with a positive image of his father, a confident, smart, and charismatic figure. And that, no doubt, helped him to become the confident, intelligent, and influential man he is today.

Lesson—*Parents, education is preparation for your child's future. Expect and accept nothing less than the best education. If you or your child is inconvenienced, so be it; that's the price you sometimes have to pay for success.*

As a single parent, do not fill your child's mind with negative images and thoughts of the other parent. It may satisfy your need for revenge, but it only serves to fill your child with self-loathing. Handle the issues with the other parent in private. Speak only of the positive, and let the child know that no matter what, the other parent loves him.

If possible, surround your child with good, supportive grandparents and other relatives. You will certainly need their help and support during the child's life. Remember, it takes a village! A child cannot receive too much love. Young Barack certainly couldn't have become the man he is today without the love and nurturing of his extended family.

Chapter 5

Successful Men in the Arts

LANCE DARDEN

Computer Animator

Salary Range: $60,000–100,000
Age: 26

Responsibilities: I am responsible for 3-D animation support at Turner Broadcasting Network (TBN). This type of work is seen in movies like *The Princess and the Frog and Finding Nemo.*

Prerequisite Skills/Traits: Drawing skills and a background in and understanding of the art of acting are very important. An animator is basically a person who does acting through an animated character. So if you are a good artist, plan to improve your skills in college or postsecondary school. There are positions available for you.

Background: I grew up in Atlanta with both my parents and my brother and sister. Yes, my father was present and helped raise me to be the man I am today. He taught me how to be a Southern gentleman. My father was a computer technician, and my mom was a schoolteacher. We definitely weren't rich by any means, but they made enough to make sure we were taken care of. My neighborhood was pretty peaceful. I grew up in a middle-class suburban neighborhood. I never saw any gang violence or things of that nature.

Natural Gifts: I wasn't exactly academically gifted, but I made good grades throughout my education. My overall GPA was around 3.5. The area that I was most gifted in was my ability to draw from a young age. That is the quality that really stood out. I was known around school as the artist. In the sixth grade, I actually designed the partnership logo between Panola Way Elementary and Wal-Mart. In high school, people paid me to draw portraits and characters for them. It was then that I realized I could use my gift to make a living for myself and be happy doing it.

Teen Years and Peer Pressure: Well, I was raised in a God-fearing environment, so that kept me pretty grounded through my teenage years. I avoided doing the wrong things because my parents taught me better. I had a very positive image in the eyes of my family and friends. My biggest challenge was probably realizing that I didn't know it all and that I had a lot to learn about being a man and handling my responsibilities. I think it hit me when my parents started making me work for the things I wanted instead of just buying them for me. It made me appreciate hard work, and it taught me good financial fundamentals like saving my money to get the things I wanted.

One of the challenges I faced in high school was the peer pressure to have sex. I know that it's even harder on kids these days, because the idea of having sex is everywhere in the media today. However, there were a few times where my friends would make fun of me because I didn't try to have sex with a girl in a particular situation. Once again, good parenting helped me overcome those situations. I knew it was wrong in God's eyes; plus, I could have got some random girl pregnant. I learned from other people's mistakes that having a baby as a teen is not a good thing. That is also the reason why I avoided having a serious girlfriend in high school.

Mentor/Greatest Influence: My mom was a huge influence in my life. She always pushed me to do my best and always encouraged me to follow my passion. She was actually the first person who put a pencil in my hand and taught me how to draw a smiley face. She taught me to keep practicing my craft until I perfected it. She would go out of her way to make sure I was going to art classes and linked me up with friends of hers who were also artists. I would not be where I am today if it weren't for her.

Advice to Parents: Both parents need to be positive influences in their child's life physically, emotionally, and spiritually.

Teach them to always follow their passion, and be supportive.

Teach your child to have a love for God and to know his word. Be spiritual leaders and examples for your kids by taking them to church every Sunday, and conduct midweek Bible studies so your kids will grow up to be strong, faithful Christians.

Advice to Boys: Currently, I am a 3-D animator at Turner Studios in Atlanta, Georgia. I would not be here today if it weren't for hard work and faith in God. After graduating from high school, I attended the Art Institute of Atlanta to pursue a degree in computer animation. During my junior year in college, there was an internship fair in which several local companies were present, including Turner Broadcasting. I was late to the internship fair, and the Turner recruiter was literally packing up her things. I pleaded with her to interview me, and she looked up at me and said, "You know you're late... right?" However, through God's grace, I managed to be the last student that she interviewed. Ironically, I was the only student in my field who received an internship that entire day. She said I was very well spoken; I displayed a lot of personality and was very passionate about my future career in animation. That internship then allowed me to network and meet professional animators and 3-D artists, who gave me a ton of advice and guidance. I then applied all the knowledge I gained from the internship... to my senior project. I graduated at the head of my class with the best portfolio in my department. Then I turned right around and contacted all the people from Turner that I networked with and landed a full-time position straight out of college. I'm the youngest and only black 3-D animator in my entire department.

I was blessed to have grown up in a household that provided an abundance of love and encouragement, which has developed me into the man I am today. However, if you weren't as fortunate, you still must follow your dreams and passions no matter what negative criticisms or influences you may have received growing up. Learn to speak proper English so you can have a conversation with anyone. You determine your own future!

OMAR RASHAD TYREE

New York Times Best-Selling Author and Speaker

2001 NAACP Image Award Recipient
2006 Phillis Wheatley Literary Award Winner for body of work in urban fiction
Salary Range: $0–500,000
Age: 45

Omar Tyree has been cited by the City Council of Philadelphia for his work in urban literacy and has published nineteen books with two million copies sold worldwide. He graduated from Howard University with a degree in print journalism in 1991. He has been recognized as one of the most renowned contemporary writers in the African-American community. He is also an informed and passionate speaker at various community-related seminars and author of urban children's books, stage plays, feature films, and songs.

Prerequisite Skills/Traits: Love of writing, creativity, vision, great oral skills

Background: My first nine years of life were spent in the hardened areas of West Philadelphia. I grew up with a single mom. My mom married when I was nine, and I grew up with a stepfather from nine years of age to eighteen. We moved to the beautiful neighborhood of Mt. Airy, where my mom worked as a pharmacist and my stepdad a welder.

Natural Gifts: Even though I was a good writer in school, I did not feel I was academically gifted. I had quality A-B grades, but I felt the pull of becoming a professional NFL player. That was what most of the African-American kids wanted to do. I had the general urban challenge of choosing the street life or an academic one, and thank God for my stepdad, I chose the academic one. Spending my teen years in Mt. Airy helped me manage peer pressure because that pull of the street life was not very prevalent.

Mentor/Great Influence: The people who were the most influential in my life were my mom and stepdad. Mom showed me the real-life ideas of hustle, determination, academic discipline, and being goal oriented. My dad showed me discipline and responsibility to get it all done.

Advice to Parents: Be in your children's lives; they need you even when they act like they don't. Be a role model that they admire because of what you stand for, and finally, remember that your children are always watching what you do. So even if parenthood gets tough, hang in there, because your child will emulate you and is looking to you for guidance. If you are a stepdad in a boy's life, don't be afraid to love and discipline him as your own. He needs you. For more on my relationship with my stepdad, read the section on "The Necessary Father."

Advice to Boys: Read, read, read! That is the name of the game. Reading opens up a world for you to enter; it improves your comprehension and concentration. It builds you into an intelligent man. It does not make you a nerd; it makes you smart and gives you options in life. Reading gives you the ultimate power. I have published nineteen books. Feel free to browse through my website at www.omartyree.com.

The Necessary Father—The Case for a Strong Father Figure

by Omar Tyree

Man, let me tell you something, at age eight, I was already a rock-headed "manchild in the Promise Land," as stated in the classic Harlem memoir from Claude Brown about growing up as an unruly black boy in America in 1940s. Only, I lived in West Philadelphia during the 1970s. But the story of my wayward youth as a black boy without the discipline of a father figure was the same. This same story has been told over and over again and from many different American households.

My mother, a pretty little thing, who graduated third from her West Philadelphia High School class in 1968, had a fetish for my tall and handsome father, Robert Tyree. Problem was Robert Tyree ran the streets and had no high school education, because he lacked a father figure to buckle him down. But it didn't matter to my mother. The good, smart, and pretty girl maintained her crush on the uneducated bad boy and got pregnant by him in her first year of college, while on an academic scholarship, no less.

Well, you know how the story goes from there. Robert Tyree was surely a tall and handsome man, but he wasn't marriage material. My mother went ahead and had his baby, which was the norm back in the late sixties, and she allowed her parents to help raise him while she went back to finish college. She then dated new men, men who were not her son's father. Some of these new men were not great character studies either. And they surely didn't want to raise another man's child.

So there I was, well fed, well clothed, and spoiled to death, because my mother was well educated and gainfully employed. Nevertheless, she needed love, and her boy needed the discipline and structure of a real father and more than just a handsome "pop" who continued to run the streets.

The next thing I knew, she had found one. His name was Melvin Alston, and he was even taller than her son's real father, and meaner, and thicker, with muscles like a football linebacker. I guess my mother simply loved herself a manly man.

Anyway, this dude actually cared more, talked to the son, played with the son, and took the son places. But once he figured out that this unruly son of hers liked to do his own thing, steal stuff, tell off grown folks, and ignore authority figures at school, Mr. Alston had a serious problem with allowing that activity to go down. So he told the son, "If you lived in my house, you would do what you needed to do when you were told to do it."

That looked and sounded like a serious threat coming from a man his size, with his West Philadelphia demeanor. But it didn't faze me at the time, because I did not live with him. And although he often came to visit, my momma and I lived in our own house. So screw him and his tough-guy talk.

Then my mother decided the unthinkable. She decided she liked this giant of a mean man so much that she wanted to marry him. What? Marry him? Well, this man showed us a new house that he wanted to buy in an area of Philadelphia called Mt. Airy, which was one of the most beautiful areas I had ever seen. Hell, I forgot all about those threats that he would put the law down on me if I lived in his house. And since my mother and I were a package deal, I moved on in and got my own room in the back.

It didn't take long for me to figure out that I had made a big mistake by letting my guard down. In fact, on their wedding night, I was so disturbed by this man's "my-way-or-the-highway" swagger, that I decided to the spend rest of that weekend at my grandmother's house. But ultimately, I had to come back and deal with this six-foot-four, two-hundred-twenty-five pound black man that my mother had married, who was now my stepfather.

Well, let me tell you, this mean man meant everything he said about having his way in his house. I ended up getting more whippings and punishments than I care to remember, but there were four incidents that were definitely wrong of me to do. Hell, I was the son of an unruly street runner. What did you expect from me? However, my mother rarely intervened to stop the discipline.

Oh, sure, she'd walk into my room and stop the onslaught of the big brown belt after I had already taken twenty licks from it, finally claiming that I had had enough. But she never stood up like the stereotypical black momma and shouted, "Oh no, you don't hit my boy! He is not your son!" No, she allowed him to be the real father that my tall and handsome pop had never been.

Outside of his obvious staunch discipline, this man, Melvin Alston, took me to tryouts for football teams, protected me, helped me with my homework, told me that I could achieve whatever I set my mind to achieve, and supported me in every way imaginable. You know, he did things that fathers are supposed to do. But since I still understood that he was not my biological father, I never bothered to call him dad, never changed my name to Alston, and I always found a way to keep my mind set on my own determined legacy. Nevertheless, the man counted me as his own son, and he did the job to raise me into a man.

Soon, he ended up having two sons of his own with my mother to tag his Alston name on to. And his sons, of course, looked at me as their big brother. Like it or not, I would have a lot of influence on them. But the track record had been set. By the time I became a teenager, I was never in any major disagreements with the law, I respected my elders, I did my schoolwork, I respected my house and my mother. I was pretty much a "good kid," and I owed it all to Mr.

Alston, because before he had come into my life, I was definitely headed toward jail for theft, violence, and a basic neglect for the laws. And it didn't matter how much education my mother had or how much she loved me.

I was a man-child who needed a man's strong hand to raise me right.

Now, that doesn't mean that I became perfect. I still had to have my own way with some things. So we struggled, my stepfather and I, through high school and even through college, on what I wanted to do, verses what he thought I should do. But you know what? Once a young son becomes more of a man, that happens in most families. The son starts to determine that he wants to live his life a different way—his way. However, no matter how I wanted or chose to live, the man's footprints were already stamped on my masculine ID.

I became a young man who would stand up for his rights, just like Melvin Alston would. I would protect and provide for my family, just like Melvin Alston had, even with a kid who wasn't his own. I would support my sons in sports, academics, and entertainment, love them, and never leave them. I also had to discipline them, although not as much as I had been disciplined, because they knew from birth what their dad was not going to stand for. And I owe all of those lessons of great fatherhood, experience, and so many good things that I picked up along the way to Mr. Melvin Alston who had done the job for me.

Now, I'm not saying that every situation is going to turn out as nicely as mine eventually did, where I can respect the job my stepfather, Melvin Alston, did to raise me. Nor am I one to hate on the lack of a job that my biological father, Robert Tyree, provided. I'm just saying that I had a personal experience that changed my life for the good, that has now become the fortunate legacy that my sons are now connected to as I continue to love them and be there for them in rock-solid family structure. And if I had to raise a stepson for whatever reason, I know just how to relate to him. Because at the end of the day, Melvin Alston understood how to love me as a little human, who was an extension of the woman that he loved. Therefore, he learned to love me as his own, through all of the difficulties on the way, while successfully raising a responsible black man in a hard culture for black men in a land called America. Thank God I had a necessary father!

Chapter 6

Successful Men in Healthcare

MICHAEL L. PENN JR. M.D.; PH.D.

Scientist/Physician

VP of Strategy, Gladstone Institutes
CEO Gladstone Foundation
Biomedical Research
Salary Range- $150,000-$300,000

Dr. Michael L. Penn Jr. graduated in 2003 from Morehouse College with a degree in biology. Later M.D. and Ph.D. from University of Southern California (USCF).The Gladstone Institutes is a biomedical research organization that studies the fundamental causes of important diseases with the ultimate goal of using this information to discover cures.

Responsibilities: Provide Leadership for strategic planning, communications and fundraising that supports Gladstone's scientific research.

Prerequisites skills/traits: College degree, drive and ambition

Background: I grew up in a black middle class home in San Francisco with both my parents. My mom was an elementary school principal and my dad worked in a variety of job, from banking at Wells Fargo to advocating for black businesses Dad was educated as well and had a Master's degree in public administration. However, he spent much time at home cooking dinner and making sure that my brother and I were well cared for. Mom's job as a principal was very demanding and even though she was not home as much as dad, we clearly knew her love, high standards and expectations. She was much disciplined, a strong authoritarian, and very encouraging. I went to private school from kindergarten through eighth grade and played all kinds of sports up until high school where my focus was tennis. Summers consisted of attending programs with academic support which I thoroughly enjoyed. I grew up in a very race conscious household, my father was a civil rights leader as a college student and marched with Dr. Martin Luther King Jr., and mom focused her dissertation study on the connection between cultural identity and self esteem of black children and the correlation with their academic achievement. She found that if children had positive and healthy feelings about their identity it lead to better outcomes in academics., So of course they were on a mission to make sure that we had high self esteem.

Physical or Emotional Challenges: I was generally considered a smart kid and schooling for me was manageable (with lots of hard work) but I had my share of challenges and embarrassment. I had very bad eczema growing up as a child. I was allergic to many foods like chocolate, corn syrup and eggs. I had to pretty much take my food with me wherever I went. I had rashes on my legs, arms, and even face -kids used to tease me constantly. I was very self-conscious about my physical body growing up.

Teen Years and Peer Pressure: Since I was very academically focused and somewhat isolated due to my parents mandate on studies, I did not succumb to the poor choices that teen sometimes make which are often influenced by peer pressure. I had direct family experience with the consequence of bad decisions. I had an uncle that was murdered by a drug dealer as well as family members who got addicted to drugs and alcohol. I also remember a significant encounter with violence – being thoroughly beaten by a kid I didn't even know. At the same time it was very traumatic but it taught me to be much more aware of my surroundings. Thankfully, this incident did not become a significant part of my life. I often felt overprotected by my parents and remember frequently feeling jealous that I did not have the same freedoms as some of my friends. I was not allowed to make decisions about where I went and what I did. My parents, particularly my mother, took her role very seriously and believed they were doing what was best for me. As an adult now, I can see the value in their approach even though I did not appreciate it back then.

College Financing: Because of my academic achievement, I had scholarships throughout my college life so my parents did not have to pay and I did not have to take out college loans. My parents helped me with a car after my freshman year. But I was very impressed with Morehouse College which also gave me a full scholarship and I thoroughly believe that I received the best education there.

Greatest Influence: Both my parents were very influential in my life. Mom was very disciplined and principled and dad was loving and giving. I believe I had the best of both worlds. But I also remember admiring my aunt and uncle who had become serial entrepreneurs. Outside of my family, I would say that I admire Nelson Mandela who dedicated his life to ending apartheid and even though he was imprisoned, he did not carry around hatred and resentment.

Advice to Parents:

1. Encourage young men to discover and embrace their unique purpose in life - the world needs each of them to contribute their greatest gifts and talents.
2. Challenge boys to take 100% responsibility for their lives. Teach them that they are inherently powerful (not victims), who can create lives for themselves that are happy, peaceful and fulfilling.
3. Show them unconditional love so they can grow up anchored in the unshakeable belief in their fundamental value as a human being with divine purpose to make a difference in the world.

Advice to Boys:

1. Have the courage to believe that you are perfect and infinitely capable of accomplishing anything. God doesn't make mistakes. Bring humility and quiet confidence as opposed to ego and bravado.
2. Trust that all of life's experience is serving your highest purpose. View challenges or obstacles as opportunities that will ultimately benefit you.

3. Be loving and compassionate to yourself and everyone you meet.

DR. DARYL SHERROD

Internist

Salary Range: $100,000–250,000
Age: 40

Responsibilities: Diagnose and treat sick patients

Prerequisite Skills/Traits: Great grades in school, bachelor's degree, MCAT, medical school (three years), residency in a hospital; be caring, hardworking, persistent, and determined

Background: I was raised by a single mother because my parents divorced when I was three years old. We lived originally in Waynesboro, Georgia, until we relocated to Atlanta after I completed the fourth grade.

I grew up in what I consider a typical middle-class family. My mom had some college and worked as a driver examiner at the motor vehicle department. I never went hungry or wanted for any of the essentials in life. Mom made sure that I had everything I needed, not everything I wanted. I remember one time we went shopping for school, and I wanted to get designer jeans. Mom gave me a choice. She told me that I could have one pair of designer jeans and one shirt, which I would wear to school every day, due to the cost, or I could get several outfits without the label. Of course I chose to have several outfits!

My neighborhood was integrated. Mom bought a house in a neighborhood that had a good school system. I was considered a latchkey kid since Mom was still at work when I got home. I would let myself in the house, lock the door, and immediately call my mom. Most of my friends were living with both mother and father, but my mother made sure that I was always in a safe environment and monitored my associations very carefully.

Challenges Growing Up: My emotional challenge growing up was being in an environment where most of my friends had mom and dad at home and I lived only with my mom. There was a slight stigma attached to that, but my dad played a big role in my life before he died. I would spend time with him and my paternal grandparents, and I know that they loved me. Mom prayed about everything, and we frequently prayed together. Her priority was for me to be the best, and you could hear the fervency in her prayers.

Natural Gifts: Yes, I believe that I was academically gifted, but I would complete my work and immediately start talking. All my teacher had to do was threaten to call my mother. (I was not physically afraid of her, but I did not want to disappoint her.) I really did not take an active interest in my education until I was in the seventh grade. It became a challenge for me to get better grades than my friends. Although I would not consider myself to be gifted, I was raised to believe that I could do anything. My mom praised and encouraged my work. Many times, she would send me "I love you" cards through the mail, telling me how proud she was of me.

Teen Years and Peer Pressure: My teen years were very busy. I remained very active in high school, and I was also a Scout leader.

The privilege there was that my scoutmaster took an interest in me and he was my mentor. I learned to do many things that helped me develop my self-esteem. The biggest challenge I can remember was being taken home by a police officer because I wrecked mom's car, the only car in the house. I wanted to die! Mom knew I had the car but facing her after I had an accident and destroyed the car was another story. Mom's surprising reaction was to ask if I was okay and hug me. Later she told me that the look of fear and disappointment in my face was enough of a punishment, so she thought I deserved a hug. She is incredible!

Peer pressure was not much of a problem because she taught me to be a leader and not a follower. She monitored my friends and acquaintances carefully. She insisted on getting a phone number of a parent to see if we would be chaperoned. Once I thought I was old enough and did not want that kind of scrutiny, and Mom did not allow me to go. I quickly learned my lesson. I think that kind of close scrutiny kept me out of a lot of trouble.

Mentor/Greatest Influence: My mother was the most influential person in my life. But there were several other people who influenced me. My scoutmaster, Earl Kitchings, made sure that I understood everything I needed to do. He took an interest in me and gave me tasks to make me feel valuable.

Advice to Parents: Three pieces of advice I would give to parents are:

1. Teach your son the value of hard work and perseverance by giving him chores. The more difficult, the better; hard work builds stamina.
2. Remind him that he is a black man and will always have to be better than his white counterpart.
3. Encourage, discipline, and praise him, as this will help him with the struggles he is sure to face.

Advice to Boys: Read and know your history. In order to move forward, you must know from where you came. Do not follow the crowd and try to be cool because too many "cool" people end up in jail. Do everything you can to excel in school; this usually paves the way for your future. Good luck, and I hope you decide to become a doctor. It's a very rewarding career, but you must stay on top of your grades. If I can do it, so can you. Good luck!

AARON SCOTT

Chief Nuclear Technologist

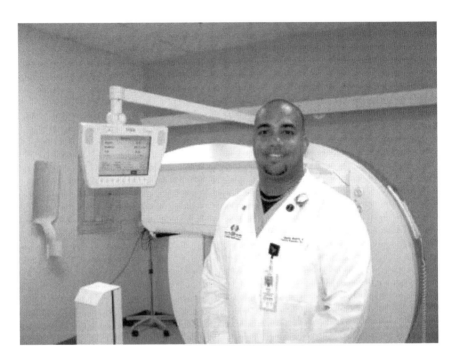

Salary Range: $60,000–120,000
Age: 38

Responsibilities: Run the entire department in nuclear technology. This would include but is not limited to performing all types of scans on patients to help determine their diagnosis.

Prerequisite Skills/Traits: One can start off as a radiology technician with an associate's or bachelor's degree and with significant experience become a supervisor. Having good communication skills and being detail oriented and able to work independently are all necessary skills. Certification is voluntary but has become more and more standard in the profession.

Background: I grew up with both my parents in a lower-middle-class home. My mom worked in the laser room at Johnson and Johnson, and my dad worked for General Motors. Mom was very strict about my education. She would make sure I did my homework as soon as I came home from school, check it for errors, and have me redo wrong ones. I thought it was her way of being mean, but I get it now and I definitely appreciate her passion for making me the best. Education was very important in our family. Both my parents saw my potential early and wanted me to take advantage of my abilities. I was allowed to have fun as long as my homework was completed well and I came in before sundown. Dad was very committed to his family. He traveled sixty-five miles (one way) every day back and forth to work.

Except for a few Asians who moved in from Laos toward the end of my high school years, the neighborhood was pretty much segregated. However, it didn't seem to bother me, because I felt secure in my environment.

Natural Gifts: I feel that I was academically gifted. My graduating class consisted of four hundred. I was one of fifteen blacks, and there were only two blacks in the honors class—myself and my cousin. I was a gifted athlete as well. I was on the varsity team in basketball, football, wrestling, and track. I hope this does not sound conceited, but I was the ultimate "hybrid." I was considered a "smart jock."

Challenges Growing Up: One of my most challenging times growing up was dealing with the death of my father at age fifteen. There was no time to grieve because I had to step into the role of helping Mom to raise my younger siblings. I was very naive about many things, including going to college. I did not have a college counselor to tell me about the application process. I really thought colleges went around and selected whom they wanted. So when I was not "selected," I tried to find a way to pay for college on my own by joining the army. This would ensure that my mom would not go into debt paying for my college.

Teen Years and Peer Pressure: Even though I was smart and popular, losing my dad, who was such a strong influence in my life, was devastating. I had the classic profile of a potential drug addict or alcoholic. I was a jock in high school, endured a major death at a critical time in my life, entered the military twice, joined a fraternity, and have been married twice. Obviously, I had been searching for something. But because I was raised never to disrespect my body, I have never tasted alcohol in my life. Yes, I did say "never." I am the guy in a club with a bottle of water in his hand. The reason is simple. No one has ever given me a good reason to start. You see, I had seen too much of what drugs and alcohol did to others, and I did not want to end up like them.

Mentor/Greatest Influence: Even though my mom made sure I was educated and I love her dearly, the person who had the most influence in my life was my dad. He was someone I always looked up to and wanted to emulate. He was my hero. He taught me right from wrong, how to treat women, how to respect my elders, and how to manage my money. The greatest lesson I learned from my dad was the difference between a life and a legacy, and I promised him at a funeral that I would leave a legacy behind. I am on that mission!

Advice to Parents:
1. Listen to your kids' dreams and goals, and do *everything* possible to help them succeed.
2. Pay attention to their friends; they are as much or even more of an influence to your child's upbringing.

3. Do not be afraid to punish them; be their parent and not their friend. Parents are responsible to teach right from wrong.

Advice to Boys (Especially African American):
1. Get an education, because it cannot be taken from you.
2. Respect women and your elders.
3. Pay attention to finances, invest, pay your bills on time, and always do your best at whatever you do.

MARCUS FIELDS

Registered Nurse

Nurse of the Year 2009

Salary Range: $60,000–100,000
Age: 37

Responsibilities: Emergency room nurse

Prerequisite Skills/Traits: Caring, patient, bachelor's degree in nursing.

Background: I grew up in the Detroit Metropolitan Area. Born in 1971, I was raised on the west side of Detroit (7 Mile/J. C. Lodge). I was raised with an older brother and a younger sister. I did enjoy having a brother and sister while growing up. The sibling rivalry is humorous when reminiscing about my childhood. I couldn't imagine being an only child. My father was present in the household until I was approximately twelve years old. I guess my parents grew apart and could not resolve their differences. I remained in constant verbal contact with my father; fortunately, he didn't move too far away. The visits were far and few between, so there wasn't what I would consider to be a real father-son relationship. I eventually moved in with him when I was a junior in high school but moved back during my senior year.

The economic circumstance that I was in was a difficult one, but there were others who were not as fortunate as our family was. My father was employed with the state in law enforcement. My mother was a stay-at-home mom until the divorce. She always had two to three jobs in an attempt to support three children and pay all the bills. I remember when she would juggle bills to make ends meet. The annual household income was low enough to qualify for government assistance (food stamps). I remember shopping at thrift stores and wearing our shoes until the soles had holes in them. I did have a great aunt who lived close by, and she provided assistance (babysitting) when she could.

Challenges Growing Up: Growing up on the west side of Detroit in the 1980s had its challenges. I grew up in a city that seemed to change for the worse right before my eyes. In the 1980s, there was major gang activity in the city, and many people died or went to jail as a result. Crime was on the rise. This seemed to be a turning point, because Detroit has never been the same—the times when neighborhoods were full of home owners (minimal vacant or abandoned homes), the lawns were manicured, and your neighbors were your friends. I was exposed to some of the more unlawful things going on in the neighborhoods while I was in middle school. It wasn't because I was a bad kid. Being in middle school just opened my eyes so I could understand better what was going on in the neighborhood. High school amplified that to the point of connecting with the east side of Detroit: the Detroit public school system.

I had no physical or emotional problems or limitations as far as I can remember.

Natural Gifts: I was considered academically gifted in certain subjects in school. Math, reading, and English were my best subjects. My father was an English major, and when he had a presence in our home, he made sure that I was reading and doing math before I even started kindergarten. I was promoted a grade while in primary school, and my brother was double promoted for the same reasons. My father was the academic enforcer prior to him divorcing my mom. My motivation for getting high grades and GPA was decreased after my parents got a divorce. It was like that unit of support was not there anymore. I did attend honors English classes in high school. I graduated as scheduled; I just wasn't the valedictorian but could easily have been.

Teen Years and Peer Pressure: I made it through my teen years with the assistance of my older brother, William. With him being only fifteen months older, I looked to him for guidance. We had a great relationship; he looked out for me like any big brother should. I was always challenged with temptations of the streets (drugs, sex, crime). I dealt with these temptations by standing firm to the morals that were instilled in me as a child from the religion that my mother practiced (Jehovah's Witnesses). I stayed away from unlawful and immoral things by working and staying busy in the community. I would hustle and make money by doing odd jobs. I was still cool with all the fellas in the hood. I had to pick and choose my associates, like any teen would.

When dealing with peer pressure, sometimes I did fold and give in.

I suggest thinking before making a decision. Ask yourself, "What are the consequences and can I deal with the consequences?" I know I've had my share of giving in to peer pressure, but I didn't do anything that was life threatening. I did have a neighborhood father figure that I would talk to and get advice from regarding certain situations. He would advise me, and I would either take his advice and use it or not. I mostly took his advice. I realized that he probably has been through what I was going through or knew a little bit more about it than me. When I was at a point in my life where I had to decide whether to go to college or not, I decided no college. I had no money, no money, and no money. I didn't know the steps to take in order to take advantage of tuition assistance, grants, and scholarships. I decided that I would go to the military for four to six years and use the GI Bill to go to college. After serving almost six years in the United States Air Force, I decided to separate myself from the armed forces and attend school. I used the military as an avenue to obtain funds for college. I used the GI Bill to pay for college, and my employer at the time had a tuition reimbursement program, which I took advantage of. If I knew then what I know now, I would have stayed in the military and let them send me to school for a job that I could do for them while in the military, and after I separated, I could use those same skills in a civilian environment (pilot, air-traffic controller, nurse anesthetist, engineer, dentist).

Mentor/Greatest Influence: I was mostly influenced by my environment. I know that I did not want to live in a situation like the one in which I grew up. I knew that I did not want to be a drug dealer or be involved in auto theft or be involved in felony robbery. I knew that I did not want to be one of the guys on the street corner drinking forty-ounce bottles of beer all day every day. I didn't want to live paycheck to paycheck or wonder where the next meal was coming from. I didn't want to live in poverty. I did, however, want to do something that was legal and that would help me live the lifestyle that I wanted. I took something good from the positive contacts I had and used that as fuel and motivation. I continue to do that even today.

Advice to Parents: Raise your son in a well-structured home. Expose your son to as much as possible. This will give him a plethora of options for hobbies and careers. Do not choose your son's career for him. Don't force him into being a basketball player or football player. Don't be demeaning if he likes rapping. Support him in his decisions and encourage him to strive for greatness. Fathers, please set the example. Your son is watching you!

Advice to Boys: You have to find what works for you. Surround yourself with positive people, network, and feed off of each other's energy. Look to those who have done it for advice. Ask questions; there are no stupid questions. Learn from others' mistakes. Educate yourself; knowledge is something that no one can take from you. No matter what, trust your gut instinct. If it doesn't feel right, it probably isn't. I have used this advice, which was given to me as a young teenager, on many occasions. It kept me out of a lot of trouble and sticky situations. Stay focused. Don't get distracted from your goals. Be a leader. Don't follow in the footsteps of others who don't share your same interest.

Chapter 7
Successful Men in Education
DR. SAMUEL TAYLOR KING

School Superintendent

Georgia Superintendent of the Year 2010–2011
Salary Range: $100,000–$400,000
Age: 48

Responsibilities: Provide administrative leadership; oversee instructional services, student support services, school-community relations, and the business and operational affairs of the school system.

Prerequisite Skills/Traits: Experience as a principal, assistant principal, and teacher; be committed and dedicated to the business of education

Background: I grew up in a very rural area in Georgia called Smithfield. We lived on a farm, and our neighbors were more than a half a mile away. I grew up with both my parents and my three brothers. My parents were both educators, who commuted many miles to work each day. My daily routine consisted of traveling with my parents to and from school, doing my homework, and working on the farm. Church and God were an integral part of my life. My father was strict and developed within us a strong work ethic. At the time, I did not appreciate it, but now I see that is what has helped me to develop into the man I am today.

Natural Gifts: Yes, I believe I was academically gifted. Learning was easy for me, and having both parents as educators, I was expected to excel and was given all the academic support I needed. There was never a question of whether I was going to college. It was just expected. At seventeen, I was happy to go away to Mercer University in Macon, and there, a whole new world opened up. My lack of social interaction was obvious. There I realized that there was so much I had to learn that I decided I would observe, study, and learn in my new environment in order to achieve my goals.

Teen Years and Peer Pressure: My life growing up was so sheltered that I did not have to deal with peer pressure. I did not stay after school since I traveled each day with my parents, and we did not have neighbors within walking distance. So my life consisted of home, school, and church. At the time, I hated not having outside friends and not being exposed to things as other people were, but I realize that even though I did not get that early socialization, it prevented some of the negative situations that may have influenced my life.

Financing College: Scholarships and loans. My parents guided me in this process. Ask your school counselor.

Mentor/Greatest Influence: The people who influenced my life most were my parents. Mom instilled values, morals, and the love of God. Dad instilled structure, discipline, and a very strong work ethic. This work ethic has been crucial in shaping my career to becoming a superintendent in a diverse school district in the South. From working in the cafeterias in college to spending my free time doing extra work in order to make our school's system one of the most successful in the country, working hard has influenced my career tremendously.

Advice to Parents: Keep a healthy family unit together (preferably mom and dad); if you are a single mom, ensure that there is a strong male role model on a consistent and persistent basis; keep him grounded in religion, moral aspects, and strong values.

Advice to Boys: Strive to live by biblical principles. Never give up! Be tenacious and resilient; if you fall down, get up quickly, brush off your pants, and move on. Become an example and role model for others. Adopt some moral standards by which to live and govern. Remember, everyone has a gift. Determine what yours is and embrace what you do as your gift. Most important, know how to humble yourself.

CHIKE AKUA

Educational Consultant, Speaker, Author

Salary Range: Teacher's salary—$40,000–$500,000

Prerequisite Skills/Traits: Experience as a teacher, being an enthusiastic speaker, and expertise in a particular area

Background: I grew up in Toledo, Ohio, the last of five children. My dad was a dentist, and my mom was a nurse. I grew up in a middle-class household, and my parents exposed me to the best of all cultures, especially the black culture. They were very socially conscious and made sure that I was aware of who I was and what I could accomplish. Up to the fifth grade, I got A's and B's in school, and I considered myself very smart. But once I entered the sixth grade, my grades started to slide. I can't put my finger on the reason even though I have done a thorough analysis of my situation, but I graduated high school with a 1.9 GPA. This is the grade average of an underachiever or someone who has not had much support, but I did not consider myself to be either. Maybe once I entered middle school, I lost all my confidence, but from sixth through twelfth grade, my grades were atrocious.

Teen Years and Peer Pressure: I was able to manage my teen years because boundaries were set by my parents. At nineteen, I was offered the chance to sell drugs, but I could not do it because I could not disappoint my parents. I remember my mom clearly saying, "These are not things we do in our house." Another thing that helped and guided me was instilling spirituality or God in the home. As a child of God, I knew this was terribly wrong, and I refused.

Mentor/Greatest Influence: The most influential people in my life were my parents. They taught me the importance of hard work and responsibility. They exposed me to the positive aspects of the African culture and to a variety of cultures. I also have to give credit to my sister, who had the patience and dedication to work with me to build up my grades at a time when those grades could not open any doors for me. She still mentors me even today.

Advice to Parents:
1. Raise the standard of expectation for your son; children rise to your expectations.
2. Restore his identity by teaching him about God, his role, and his importance in the family.
3. Reform his daily routine; make sure he has a daily routine that keeps him busy and challenged. Monitor what your child is doing on a daily basis. You don't need to live in a middle-class environment for this to happen. You need to have a vision for your child and be conscious and committed. Look at Ben Carson. His mom was a maid, but she made sure he read books and required him to do a book report every week. A whole new world opened to him once he started reading.

Advice to Boys: "It's your world." You determine what your world will be. You determine what you will revolve around and what will revolve around you. Will you follow excellence or underachievement? Will you be cool today and become a fool tomorrow? You create your world by your own thoughts followed by your actions. If you know how to speak to adults by being respectful, adults will open doors for you. It is all about your attitude!

DORRIAN RANDOLPH

Teacher

Salary Range: $35,000–100,000
Age: 34

Responsibilities: Teach, grade papers, prepare lesson plans, collaborate with colleagues and the administration, communicate with parents, attend workshops, manage the classroom effectively, be a mentor

Prerequisite Skills/Traits: Bachelor's degree, caring, dedicated, patient, love children

Background: I grew up in St. Pete, Florida, with both my parents until they split when I was in seventh grade. From there, my brother, sister, and I had to decide who we would like to live with. We all chose our mom because we wanted to stay in the familiar neighborhood. After I got into some unfortunate circumstances in tenth grade, I was forced to move in with my dad for my own betterment. I say "forced" because my only two options were to move to the juvenile detention center (JDC) or with my dad. I believe the choice was an easy one to make. In a nutshell, my dad was always there *even though I did not live with him at all times.*

Our economic circumstance, I believe, was that of lower middle class. We didn't have a lot of money for me to have all the things that I thought I wanted, but we did have enough money to survive. My mother was the activity assistant/ administrative assistant for the elderly at the nursing home. My father was a manager at Checkers and then was promoted to district manager for the same franchise.

The neighborhoods that we lived in were HUD houses or apartments. We didn't have a lot of money, so we did need some government assistance. We moved a few times within the same neighborhood; sometimes, we lived in a house, and sometimes, we lived in an apartment. The neighborhood was pretty stable, and crime was low; the biggest problem was peer pressure.

Natural Gifts: I was labeled or tagged gifted. Back then, you could be considered gifted but then could have that tag snatched from you at anytime you didn't display that gift anymore. I was labeled gifted in fourth grade. I was at Pasadena Elementary. I was in fourth and fifth grade at the same time. After that school year, I went to sixth grade. I did two years in one. Throughout middle school, I was always in AP classes, which are advanced placement classes. In high school, I started to slack off because I was trying to fit in, so that gifted label was removed. I did get my act together to graduate with a 3.4 grade point average.

Peer Pressure and Teen Years: Trust me when I say that even with the pressures that parents go through, it is nothing compared to the pressure of teenage years. They were actually my toughest years. I recall one particular time that was the most challenging for me; it was in the last days of school in ninth grade. I attended a majority white school, and on the last day of school, they [the blacks kids] had a ritual where they would pick out a white kid, walk up to him, start a conflict, and then out of the blue punch him in the face and run off to the bus. This particular day was to be my last day of school in high school. I was with my friends when they started the ritual, and then they ran to their buses. Since I wasn't a bus rider, I walked home. As I was walking through the parking lot heading home, I was cornered by the campus and county police about an assault. The victim told the cops that I'd hit him. That was totally false, but since I was around to witness it and I was the only black face left on campus, he blamed me. I ended up going to court for assault and was about to be found guilty when my mother got her chance to stand up and testify/plead my case. The judge felt sympathy for my mom and agreed to send me away to my father for a year. I never told on my friend, and he got off free—no punishment—while I had to move away. In hindsight, my friend never paid the consequences for his action, and in the long run, that didn't help him because he was used to getting away with bad behavior. Now my friend is in prison for murder and is currently serving twenty-five years for stabbing someone to death.

Handling or learning how to handle peer pressure may be the hardest thing to do as a kid growing up. I was fortunate enough to have my parents to help guide me through some situations. Unfortunately, there are going to be times when you must handle them alone depending on your situation. But with strong family support and a good set of friends, I was able to handle most peer pressure situations. My parents always gave me advice on how to handle certain situations, which were hot topics for teens at the time. Yes, I even had to move because I ended up making the wrong choice during that one high school moment.

Financing College: I was able to pay for college a variety of ways. I used different resources. I used academic and football scholarships to help pay my way. I also used grants and loans to pay for my schooling. I suggest you do research to get scholarships, because you don't have to pay those back. Any loans you take out, you have to pay back when you graduate college. Definitely, keep your grades up so you will qualify for some of the academic scholarships that are out there because there are a lot of them. Keep your options open always.

Mentor/Greatest Influence: Depending on my stage of life, I had many different influences. Most supportive were my parents. They were always there for me even though they weren't together. They simply kept me grounded, and I saw how hard they worked to make us feel like a normal family. For that, they get a round of applause. My mom was a young teenager, but she did everything in her power to give me a solid childhood. It was my social studies teacher Kathryn Geraghty, my math teacher Tammy Richardson, and my football coach Michael Morey who kept me alert and on my toes throughout my high school years. In college, my football coaches

Fred Franklin and Derek Scott kept me grounded and focused. They encouraged and supported me.

Advice to Parents:
1. Always talk to your children about everything, because times have changed and even though your child may not act like it, he needs you now more than ever. So always keep that line of communication open.
2. Have a good line of communication with the teachers in your child's life, because believe it or not, kids tell teachers and teachers see more than you do. For some reason, kids will tell teachers their inner secrets before they tell their parents, so you should have that line open to find out things your child doesn't tell you.
3. Keep restrictions and boundaries between the parent/child and the parent/friend relationship. I see a lot of times that parents are treating their children as their friends or equals, and that causes lots of problems. They must know when you're being the parent and when you are being their friend. I have to do it as a teacher; my students know when I'm being serious and when I'm joking and having fun.

Advice to Boys:
1. Choose your friends wisely because in those times of peer pressure, you will need someone on your side to recognize

when something isn't right not be afraid to let you know. Sometimes the "homeboys" in the neighborhood aren't the best friend candidates especially if they are the type that are constantly in trouble.
2. Be a leader and not a follower.
3. Don't be afraid to be different from the norm. What I mean by this is you do not have to do what everyone else is doing. If everyone around you has sagging pants, you shouldn't. Try pulling your pants up and wearing them on your waist. Try changing your style of dress. My dad always told me that the one that stands out is the one that is doing something different. Remember that!

I came from the ghetto, as it is referred to today, and I made it. It was not a smooth road either. I took my share of bumps and bruises, but I got up and kept moving. I faced peer pressure and made some wrong decisions. I paid the consequences for my actions, but most important, I learned from those mistakes and vowed to never make them again. I don't believe in making the same mistake twice. I had a strong, supporting cast of friends, parents, teachers, and coaches. Ultimately, we as young black males are going to have to grow up a little faster in life so we don't end up in one of the two places that America has for us to go and that is jail or the cemetery. If you don't get anything but one thing from my story, let it be this: you are not going through anything I haven't been through and I made it. I consider myself a successful male, because I educate young minds every day and I see the positive impact I make in their lives daily. I wouldn't trade that for anything else in the world! Now it's your turn to show someone else it can be done!

DR. STEPHEN APPEA

School Principal

Salary Range: $120,000–$150,000
Age: 40

Responsibilities: Oversee the overall educational, financial, personnel, and safety operations of a school with 780 students in three academies (primary, elementary, and middle school); one hundred employees; and a six million-dollar budget

Prerequisite Skills/Personality Traits: Diligent, hardworking, persistent, ambitious

Background: I grew up in Ghana, England, and Canada before moving to Brooklyn, New York, at sixteen. My parents, who were both teachers, separated when I was about ten and divorced a few years later. I had very little contact with my father from about age twelve on.

After my first two years in high school, my mother thought I was hanging around with kids whose aspirations were not what she wanted for her son and enlisted the help of my grandmother, who helped raise the tuition ($10,000 per year in 1977 was a lot of money!) to send me to an exclusive all-boys boarding school along the Vermont-Quebec border. For the most part, these students were from the Canadian and American elite upper middle class. Yet, I'll never forget the first word any boy spoke to me: "Nigger in the hall!" When everyone realized that regardless of our different skin colors, we were pretty much similar, most of the racial issues subsided. Though I do recall enrolling in a taekwon-do class after getting beat up by a bigger and stronger

Caucasian boy. (Ironically, he enrolled in the same class after I got an older and bigger boy to beat him up!) Boarding school was life changing, as it developed my independent functioning and broadened my horizons. Although I was not from a poor family, we certainly weren't rich. At school, however, in many cases, I rubbed shoulders with boys who were from some very privileged homes. For example, one of my roommates (at that time, the only other black student in the school) was chauffeured in a private jet and Rolls Royce to and from his holiday destinations. Another one of my roommates' fathers owned twenty to thirty office buildings in a nearby city.) The school featured a Spartan vision of education involving strict physical discipline (I still have scars on my back from the beatings they gave me; at that time in that environment, corporal punishment was legal) and high academic and athletic expectations. Although most students were from well-to-do families, one's worth was determined by one's grades and athletic, extracurricular, and leadership accomplishments. As a result, I had a very well-rounded liberal arts and physical education with a lot of competitive sports travel built in to the weekend schedule leaving little downtime. While at various points I was the captain of the JV [junior varsity] basketball, soccer, and ice hockey teams, I was exposed to a wide variety of sports training (e.g., track, squash, field hockey, tennis, and golf). Non-sports weekend recreation often featured going back and forth across the American and Canadian borders without an adult chaperone.

The formative academic and extracurricular experiences of high school, together with the development of independence and self-discipline, served me well in my college and postgraduate years. In hindsight, my mother's decision to send me to boarding school was a critical formative event, which might be a recommended step for parents whose boys have little way out of a limiting environment.

Both of my parents were college educated and became teachers. For most of my childhood, I would have been considered upper middle class in Ghana and middle class in England, Canada, and the United States.

Although most people would not characterize us as rich, until I came to Brooklyn, New York I never lived in an apartment, so there was always the idea in my mind that when one grew up one should get a job, save money, and buy a house with land. I've lived in rural, suburban, and urban environments in all four countries in which I grew up.

Natural Gifts: When my parents moved from Ghana to Canada, it was determined that I should skip the first grade. As a result, I was always one of the youngest in my classes throughout the rest of my academic career. I usually excelled at reading and writing activities. I was usually an above-average student throughout school, though almost never at the top, mostly because I was rarely motivated enough by school to give it 100 percent. It was only in graduate school that I started being motivated more by a desire for excellence than by a mild fear of failure.

I was blessed to be free of any physical challenges and able to be competitive athletically. In fact, it was this athletic talent that helped me to deal with the emotional issues I experienced as a result of the dysfunction in my family.

Teen Years and Peer Pressure: One of the troubles I had as a teen was making choices to avoid friends who I knew were doing drugs. One strategy I used was to develop other serious hobbies like sports, chess, music, and reading. These naturally led me to friends who were more interested in less-destructive habits.

College was actually a positive peer experience for me because at McGill University during the early to mid-eighties, only about 1 percent of students were of African descent. As result, many of us knew each other and associated with each other as minorities within a larger society. I joined a number of student organizations and found like-minded individuals of all races, but my favorite memories are ones involving the South Africa Committee (in those days, there was a large international student movement to end apartheid in South Africa) and the Black Students Network. As it turned out, many of these former college friends and associates eventually pursued graduate degrees and became attorneys and politicians.

Graduating from college wasn't really an option for me! It was rather merely a step, and it was a very clear expectation that I would obtain a graduate degree. (In fact, there really was never even any celebration in my family that I had finished my bachelor's, maybe a few smiles and pats on the back.) Nor was there an expectation that my parents would pay for college, as there seems to be these days. I usually worked throughout the year, and I usually had three jobs in the summer and saved my money so that with careful spending, I could last for most of the year. Near the end of the spring semester, I usually ate a lot of spaghetti. I remember one semester where for several weeks, I ate only pasta. If I wanted to spice it up, I added pepper, salt, and ketchup.

Mentor/Greatest Influence: Clearly, it was my mother who played the biggest role in my childhood and teenage years. She sacrificed everything for her children, and I, being the oldest, reaped many benefits, most notable perhaps is the gift of responsibility. By being the "man of the house" before I was a man, I learned how to balance the work of family chores and babysitting with doing my own schoolwork and part-time jobs.

Advice to Parents: Develop a natural gift, talent, or ability in your child. For many boys, this may turn out to be something athletic for social and biological reasons. Even though I was a talented high school athlete and musician, when I was sixteen to seventeen, I spent many more hours playing chess, and it was this love of and devotion to chess that helped keep me out of trouble at a crucial time. It also helped develop my ability to self-discipline, self-regulate, and to focus. During one point of 1979, I was the number three–ranked junior player in the city of Montreal.

Help your son develop a positive peer group. It's important that his friends reinforce values similar to your own. It's no surprise that the students in the high school chess club, of which I was the captain, all graduated from college and pursued advanced degrees in engineering and medicine. In fact, it is actually surprising that in spite of the fact that I later minored in physiology in college, I was the only one in that close-knit high school chess club peer group (of mostly Asians and Jews) who didn't become a medical doctor, engineer, or architect.

Advice to Boys: One piece of advice for a teenage African-American male would be: find something positive that you are passionate about and find friends who are also interested in this activity as well as an adult mentor to help develop your ability and to guide you when necessary.

One of the experiences that helped me throughout my life was joining the debate club in high school. I still remember the pride I felt after winning a spot on the debate club team's trip to the North American High School debating championships in Manhattan. After the competition, in which we did well but did not actually win, I celebrated by going to a restaurant and ordering lobster with thirty dollars that I had saved myself and which in the late seventies was a lot of money for a fifteen-year-old kid! Over and over again later in life, people would comment on how well I spoke. Is it any surprise that now, thirty years later, I make my living with the words I speak? Find something that you are passionate about; something that is productive, legal, and in which you can find a mentor to guide you. Then practice, practice, and more practice! In the words of Jesse Jackson, "If your mind can conceive it and your heart can believe it, then you can achieve it."

Chapter 8

Successful Men in Business

HEZEKIAH GRIGGS III

Entrepreneur, President, and CEO, HG3

Salary Range: Multimillionaire
Age: 21

Responsibilities: CEO of daily operations of HG3, speaker, and motivator

This twenty-one-year-old has been the recipient of more than three hundred awards and recognition from organizations nationwide. Former President Bill Clinton also honored his contribution and dedication to young people.

Background: I grew up with my mom in Passaic, New Jersey. My father was not active in my life, so I grew up in poverty and at one time became homeless. From a young age, I was extremely mature. I consider myself a "peculiar kid," because even though I grew up in extreme poverty, I never saw the poverty, but I saw my neighborhood as being deprived and I noticed that there were needs to be filled.

So at age sixteen, I decided to start my own company. I am now chairman and president of HG3, a multimillion-dollar enterprise managing twenty different corporate operations and forty-five collective media properties. I thrive on hard work, and so I am also chairman of the Hezekiah Griggs Foundation, where I provide valuable assistance to community youth programs throughout the New York, New Jersey, and Connecticut tristate area as well as tools and resources needed for young people to survive in the twenty-first century.

Teen Years and Peer Pressure: I was faced with challenges of a mature man when I was still a teenager. After all, I was running a company and had to deal with CEOs of large corporations. This type of challenge was difficult but made me stronger. I did not have a typical teenage-hood because I was so focused on solving life's problems that I did not spend time with teenagers. My time was spent trying to convince corporations of the problems and getting them to support my cause.

Advice to Parents:

1. Don't try to teach him to be a man.
2. Allow your son to make mistakes but be supportive.
3. Understand how your actions influence your child before you correct his mistakes. Remember, it is not what you say, but what you do.

Advice to Boys:

1. Understand that you are the most important person.
2. Understand your purpose and do what you believe and know.
3. Use self-discipline, be decisive, that means making the right decision when presented with a choice... then you honor yourself.

I try not to wallow in despair, but I look forward to dealing with life's problems. Life is all about how you deal with problems. Learn from your mistakes and become wise, because if you don't, you will remain a fool.

RICHARD B. JEFFERSON, ESQ.

Entertainment Attorney, M·E·T·A·L· Law Group, LLP

Salary Range: $100,000 up (no ceiling since I am a partner with my firm)
Age: 37

Responsibilities: I provide legal representation for people and companies in the media, entertainment, technology, action sports (i.e., mixed martial arts), and lifestyle brands (i.e., healthy products) industries. This can include forming and maintaining their companies, protecting their copyrights and trademarks, negotiating deals, representing them in lawsuits, or just giving legal advice so that they make informed decisions.

Prerequisite Skills/Traits: Bachelor's degree, law school (three years), pass state bar

Since I am a partner, I make money on whatever work I do, so there is no cap on income. Of course, if there is no work, then the bottom range is zero.

Background: I grew up with both parents in the household. Both parents worked a lot (which was typical), so I spent a lot of time in organized activities to keep me out of trouble (i.e., sports, music, work). My father passed away when I was eighteen.

When I was very young, we had a meager economic situation. My parents were young teachers, which didn't pay much yet demanded long hours. As time passed, my parents moved up the ranks and our economic status improved. I would say that we were close to average black middle class by the time I was in twelfth grade.

Similar to our improved economic status, we moved a few times... beginning in areas that were considered less desirable to mainstream society (predominately black) to decent areas (racially mixed, country) to a nice middle-class, black area by high school. Each area taught me a lot, so I didn't have any problems with them.

Natural Gifts: I was capable of being in advanced classes throughout education. There were some hurdles that prevented me from excelling as fast as I could have (i.e., financial issues where we couldn't afford the tools to be in the advanced classes or programs, racial incidents—particularly, I remember having the best math scores in seventh grade, yet the teachers demoted me to a remedial math class in eighth grade) but I discovered that hurdles are a part of life (and you have extra hurdles to jump when you are a black male).

Challenges Growing Up: If you call having a hard-nosed, old-school father an emotional challenge...yes!

Teen Years and Peer Pressure: I was always one who constantly had to balance my desire to excel in academics with trying to stay "cool." My father helped me stay focused on the academics, because I was not permitted to have fun or play sports if I brought home a B—(he actually frowned on anything lower than an A-). Looking back, my parents' expectations instilled the morals and drive that lasted long after my teen years. I, of course, got into some mischief and situations that I knew were wrong, but after I did, I was able to pull myself out of such and get back on track. In short, my parents gave me a conscience that self-evaluates my actions to this day. I think that is what is missing from some of the youth today, and it is not their fault... This needs to be instilled by the parents or guardians.

As I alluded earlier, my father was very strict, and he did what he felt was necessary to raise a young black boy in the uncertain society of the seventies and eighties. When peer pressure came my way, it wasn't hard to deal with because I knew that if I engaged in something too extreme (like constantly skipping school, which some of my peers did), I would have hell to pay in my house. Specifically, I remember when everyone (guys) was getting one ear pierced to look cool. I could have followed that trend but at what cost... being kicked out of the house? Those types of things became less important to me, and I handled them by convincing myself I was "cool" and unique because I was the only one who didn't have my ear pierced. I basically just became analytical about peer pressure situations and did what I wanted. What other people said did not affect me (and actually if people tried to taunt me, I became motivated to show them why their decision was wrong).

Mentor/Greatest Influence: Definitely my father. I mention him a lot above, but after his passing, I reflected on how motivated he was in his life, and it helped me understand that his actions were more influential on me than his words. If a door closed in his face, he just adjusted his focus (i.e., we moved) and kept moving forward towards his goal. That is a key lesson to learn because there are always going to be obstacles or brick walls in life. The only way to achieve your goal is to move around (adjust your path) or bust through them. It is also important to know when to do one or the other.

Also, moving around (I lived in three different cities, went to a few different high schools) and being forced to adapt definitely influenced me. It taught me how to be independent and interact with new people.

Advice to Parents:
1. Strictly enforce the value of traditional education. To be successful and to maintain success, education is imperative.
2. Instill strong morals and values. You will not be around your son most of the hours of his life (i.e., day care, school, when he is with friends, etc.). He needs to know the difference between right and wrong.
3. Encourage nontraditional education. There is much more to life than traditional education. Find out what interests your son and give him the opportunity to learn from the best person you can find who is doing that activity (e.g., musician, artist, attorney, etc.).

I think the overall most important thing to do is keep your son busy with productive activities so he does not have time to find trouble.

Advice to Boys: Black males have to understand that we not only have to deal with the trials and tribulations that life presents all males, but we have yet one more obstacle to deal with: society's negative outlook on black males. We also do not get the occasional breaks that other males in society may get (e.g., if we get pulled over by the police, we are going to get a ticket no matter what we say, where another race may be able to reason with the police). My wise grandfather told me to never depend on getting the benefit of the doubt. Always do what is right and legal, and although that is a harder route, you cannot be stopped. Basically that means, do not take shortcuts even if other males do and get away with doing them (e.g., drunk driving) because as a black male, you are always being watched and scrutinized, and you will be the one who pays for the consequence.

Black males have to be tough and intelligent to become successful.

MAURICE HURST

Electrical Engineer

Salary Range: $50,000--$104,000
Age: 53

Responsibilities: Licensed professional engineer with power utility company. Design protection and control systems for power transmission substations in various Georgia locations. Mentor designers, junior engineers and serve on different committees to enhance safety in the workplace.

Prerequisite skills/traits: Although math and science is an important skill in my job, creativity and communication helps engineers to design and share their ideas with others. I was not the best math and science student, but I really liked creating new things and helping people. I worked hard to learn math and science. I learned from my parents that these skills, in addition to public speaking and writing, was very important to succeed.

Background: I grew up in Illinois and Michigan, with my family. My mother and father provided for and protected my two sisters and me, with love and discipline and a middle class lifestyle. Family was and still is important to us, which included grandparents, cousins, aunts and uncles. My father was raised by both his parents in Illinois. My parents and grandparents were great examples to follow as I raised my own two children.

My father was a school teacher before becoming an FBI agent. My mother worked in retail stores to help support our family. We had a middle-class lifestyle, but they saved on groceries, cars and homes to do it. My sisters and I were never hungry, except between meals.

We did not have name-brand clothes, but we were always clean and neat. We were raised to think for ourselves and follow our own dreams, while being respectful of family and others. This outlook prevented us from wasting our money and time while trying to impress our friends. True friends are not impressed by clothes, but by trust and character. My parents are now retired and live a good life.

We grew up in several cities, East St. Louis, Chicago IL and also Detroit MI. Although these were different cities, we lived in similar neighborhoods. My parents were determined to raise their family in safe, suburban neighborhoods so that my sisters and I could enjoy life in good schools and around good people. I played football, baseball, wrestling and track. In Illinois, it was cold enough to ice skate outside. I was also involved in Boy Scouts.

Natural Gifts: I was not academically gifted, but I had a family that depended on me to do my best. So I tried to live up to their expectations.

Challenges Growing Up: I did not have any physical or emotional challenges, but I had friends who had alcohol addictions and emotional problems that stemmed from family problems. I tried to accept them for who they were and the problems they faced, without falling in their plight and embarrassing my family. My biggest challenge as a teen, came from my own parents, though.

During my second year in college and away from home, my girlfriend and I got pregnant with our daughter. I was nineteen. I was more heart-broken when I disappointed my family than I was afraid of this new and huge responsibility. I did not hesitate to marry my girlfriend, even though they thought that was ruining my chances to graduate from college and succeed. I proved them wrong, although I never said that to them. I knew that my family loved me and expected me to make right decisions, but they also taught me to be my own leader, to make up my own mind and not be a follower. I believe that I did okay, in the end. However, I highly suggest that good men abstain from sexual activity until they marry and are better able to support a family. It was easy to get in trouble when I was a teen. It is even easier now to get in trouble with alcohol, drugs, sexual activity and stealing. I also tried to avoid trouble because I knew I would get punished when I got home. My parents were not afraid to discipline me.

Teen Years and Peer Pressure: I got through my teen years with very few problems because I was kept out of trouble by all the family members around me. First, I had a GOD who I knew expected me to make right decisions. I lived in neighborhoods where most families were determined to live right. I had a large family that included many adults who worked hard to provide for their children and elderly. Sure, I made mistakes, but they were not so bad that I could not be forgiven or corrected. I was involved in church, even when I went off to college, because I felt accountable to those who were important to me. I wanted to be trusted. I realized that I could not be trusted when I made friends who could not be trusted.

For the most part, I managed peer pressure by getting friends who wanted to do right. Any boy or girl, with a good family, could get into trouble by hanging out with the wrong crowd. I raised my own children to pick their friends wisely, because they will make decisions, good or bad, because of who is important to them.

Financing College: As I said earlier, I got married early in life so I had to pay for my own college. I worked several jobs to support a family and pay for school. I was a taxi driver, janitor, restaurant manager, technician, bank guard and pizza deliverer. I even enlisted in the United States Marine Corps to make money and save for college. I also got help from my parents, even though I was determined to succeed as the leader of my own household. I graduated from North Carolina State College, after attending two junior colleges, with no college loans. It is much easier to attend and pay for junior college, then later graduate from a large university. There is far less distractions at smaller schools and teachers work harder to help students succeed.

Mentor/Greatest Influence: GOD was and is the most influential person in my life. After HIM, my family is most influential to me.

When I was a teen trying to stay out of trouble, I often considered my parents and sisters in my decisions. My father's parents died when I was only ten years old, and my mother's mother lived with us in her old age. She always told me that, "you are going to make it" in this world. I remembered that. She was a great inspiration to me. Later, when I had a family of my own, I considered my childrens well-being and their respect for me. I am influenced by them, in making my decisions, because I wanted them to always be proud of me. My first marriage did not last. However, in due time, God found another wife for me and I am truly thankful for her. I will continue to be influenced by God and family, This is a valuable lesson... wait on the Lord, the cost is too high when you buy too early.

Advice to Parents: Being a successful black man requires work, sacrifice, self-discipline and accountability. Raising successful black men requires work, sacrifice, self-discipline and accountability. Parents cannot teach success unless they are good students of these four attributes. Parents make mistakes, including serving themselves before their family and also trying to be a friend to their children. Children watch their parents and even know when they are not acting responsibly. Children expect the best of their parents, not the best from their parents. Children want and need a loving and responsible model to follow along the way to adulthood. As the BIBLE says, "train up a child in the way he should go...", the trainer must lead the way. Finally, parents must be willing to seek forgiveness for their many mistakes and to teach their children to be responsible for their good and bad decisions.

Advice to Boys: The first of three pieces of advice that I would give to young black boys and men: Be a man and not just a male. Humans are more than just males and females. A boy or young man's decisions in life should be determined by whether he is a man, a good man, or just a male. Men do manly deeds; males do only male deeds. Secondly, accept responsibility for your own actions and not the bad decisions of your friends. So pick your friends wisely. I love the poem by an unknown author, "The Test of a Man". It describes a good model of responsibility to follow, for all young men. Finally, find respectable people to be accountable to. We often make poor decisions when we think no one knows or does not care. But in reality, at least GOD knows and HE does care. Try not to disappoint HIM, or your family.

W. ANTHONY DRUMMOND

Entrepreneur, Certified Public Accountant, Hotel Owner, Author

Mr. Drummond seen with his great grandson Jonah and some boys in his mentoring program.

Salary Range: $100,000–$500,000

Age: 80

Background: I grew up with both my parents in a poor rural area on the island of Jamaica. I was the first of twelve to survive, and so my parents were very protective of me. My other siblings had died from childhood diseases that were prevalent at that time. My dad was very patient in teaching me to form letters as a child, but my mom was the typical matriarch; she made things happen. She was a go-getter and made sure the impossible became possible.

I loved school and never accepted second place in class. I always wanted to be first. As a child growing up in the deep country, I did not have toys, except the ones I made out of sticks. My fondest memories were those of my dad helping me to form letters and write in cursive when he came home from the field. He was a local farmer, who would always compliment me with "good boy" when I was able to get things correctly.

Natural Gifts: Yes, I must say I was academically gifted, but I also had my share of setbacks. Shyness, stuttering, and being of short stature were impediments in my mind, and so I worked extra hard to be seen and heard. I would always sit in the front of the room, raise my hands to answer questions, and make sure my work was impeccable. Being in high school and living in poverty was not really an asset, but I learned to camouflage my lack of things by being smart. As a grown man, I now see that having those humble beginnings made me appreciate things much more.

Mentor/Greatest Influence: I think my dad played the most influence in my life, but my mom made things possible for me. She was the one to meet with teachers, speak on my behalf, and right things in my life when they were wrong. She was the ultimate "matriarch" and is responsible for what I am today. I thank her for her devotion to me and my siblings. The attention my dad paid to me though was priceless. The look of pride in his eyes, the hugs, and the patience he showed me as a boy gave me strength and courage as an adult.

Advice to Parents:
1. It is important for dads to stay involved in their children's lives. (That was one of the mistakes I made in my life.)
2. Moms should allow a competent dad to be able to teach boys the ways of manhood.
3. Love your children unconditionally and show them you care, another mistake I made earlier in my life.

Advice to Boys: Believe in yourself. Do not let your size, your speech, or any physical handicaps get in your way. Aim for the best. I had to overcome size and speech problems, but I believed in myself and I pushed forward. You can do it; you have no choice. You are a male, and as a man, women look to you for leadership. You need to be strong and intelligent. You need to look in the mirror and be proud of yourself. This takes discipline. Study hard, and work hard. If you are not academically gifted, do your best and be the best at what you do. You know you are successful when you do what you do well. Remember, as a man, you must lead, and in order to do that, you need to be confident, knowledgeable, and disciplined.

Mr. Drummond is the author's father who passed away during the writing of this book.

Chapter 9

How Important Should Sports Be in Your Son's Life?

JULANI GHANA SPORTS MANAGER

Sports Manager

Julani Ghana seen here with Eric Snow who played for the Cavaliers
Salary Range: $50,000–150,000
Age: 48

Responsibilities: Manage the personal and business affairs of high profile professional athletes, entertainers, and public figures as well as connecting them to the greater community for greater leverage and a lasting legacy.

Prerequisite Skills/Traits: Strong leadership roles throughout the school experience, bachelors and masters degrees in the following areas: business, communications, public relations, sports management, marketing along with experience and strong community networks. Other important skills include, a high degree of creativity, strong oral and written skills, problem solving, event planning, a high degree of integrity, the ability to work successfully under high degrees of stress and pressure, a strong understanding of the non-profit and community education industries, the ability to work with extreme confidentiality and anonymity, must be able to travel, demonstrate strong organizational skills, and work long non-traditional hours.

Background: My whole life revolves around a distinct understanding that knowledge was the key to power and getting a good education was the key ingredient to acquiring vast amount of knowledge. My parents drilled in all of us children that whatever power was accumulated through this process was not ours to keep. We were duty bound to share it with others in our community and to use it as a means to elevate ourselves and others.

Because of the unique history of African people in America, access to the traditional forms of social, economic, educational, employment opportunities were very limited. My parents came from very humble beginnings. My mother was a Hall of Fame and 3-letter athlete in our hometown as well as a high school graduate. However, there weren't many colleges calling to help her get into college. Her being pregnant with my oldest sister did not help matters much.

My father migrated north from the Black & Native American regions of Virginia's eastern shore. Though he was a standout neighborhood athlete, he never finished high school. He went into the work force very early and focused much of his life on being a devoted father and husband.

Both of my parents stressed hard work, the responsibility of learning and enhancing Black culture, community service and strong participation in sports as the means to elevating one's position in life.

Their insistence in our participation in sports as a training ground for a "unique yet profound" understanding of the complexities of racism, Black culture, and self-actualization has always been the foundation for my life. Through sports I learned the lessons of life by watching and reading the stories of Black sports legends and human rights activists such as Paul Robeson, Jackie Robinson,

Arthur Ashe, Muhammad Ali, Pele', Roberto Clemente, Bill Russell, along with Curt Flood, Althea Gibson and Black Power duo Tommy Smith and John Carlos.

Challenges Growing Up: One of the greatest challenges I faced as a adolescent was trying to understand the power and complexity of major issues such as racism, poverty, and hopelessness while being raised in a northeast suburban Philadelphia community as opposed to an underserved urban neighborhood or growing up in the deep South. Our financial situation on paper was very tough yet as children, we really did not realize how poor we were until we met kids from outside of the community. Moreover, our understanding of America, racism, and the distinct advantage that white kids had over us was marred in the reality that there were few daily major incidents of overt racial confrontations. In my hometown, it seemed as if everyone got along. However through sports, we were able to clearly recognize the distinct differences in the treatment and expectations of Black players. My father taught me a "distinct science" of how things work in America and was able to articulate his points through my participation in sports. It shaped my understanding of the world and helped me recognize that through sports, I possessed a major vehicle by which I could elevate my personal situation and also change the world.

Natural Gifts: I was a superb athlete and had always been strong in the traditional areas of athleticism: running, jumping, quick reflexes, and coordination. But where I really stood out from others (I believe) was sort of a natural leadership and boldness that accompanied me in sports and in the classroom. I sort of just took the lead in most instances and people just followed. I enjoyed the idea of leading and helping others succeed. I think a lot of those athletic gifts were inherited from my mother. Going through her yearbook, I marveled at the fact that she excelled in sports and had quite the reputation. My father, though very adept in sports, operated like a world historian and social scientists. He was not interested so much in leading any type of movement. Instead, he focused on teaching all of his children a profound understanding of the way things worked for Blacks in America and what was possible. I had a natural proclivity for history and speaking that came from my father. I gravitated easily towards his lessons. My father always encouraged to learn our history and to always express our thoughts. We sort of had a mandate to always challenge the status quo after recognizing, acknowledging, and understanding it even existed.

Teen Years and Peer Pressure: The younger years of my youth were consumed with sports and understanding the seemingly invisible nature of race relations. As a superior athlete, I had amazing access to people, places, and things. It wasn't long before I noticed others did not have that same access they looked like me and came from my same neighborhood. Sports granted me uncanny glimpse of what America looked like for others. I got used to being named captain or president on most of my sports teams, civic groups, or just in the neighborhood. I also had great role models in my two older sisters. Both were multiple sport stars and loved by the larger community. They set the tone for me and my brother who would come on later as a local sports star in his own right. In the end sports eliminated the type of anxiety that regular young guys experienced as it even granted me access to tough neighborhoods with a passport not given to others. Because of the reputation and access acquired through sports, there was rarely any pressure to conform to any activities that did not involve excellence in sports like drugs, fighting, illegal activities, poor grades, or even risky behaviors involving girls.

Mentor/Greatest Influence: I have dedicated most of my life's work as a tribute to my parents. Their incredible sacrifice is the motivation by which I try and attain the greatest heights. I did not have to look far for great role models and between the two of them along with my sisters, and a number of very high character and successful neighbors as well as relatives (especially Black men), I found most of what I needed right in my general circle.

However, like most young people, there is always that search outside for validation of our parents' teachings. I discovered confirmation through a man named Joseph Sessoms. Coach

Sessoms (as we called him since he was also a football coach) had taught my two older sisters and would later teach both me and my younger brother. He was a math teacher and the FIRST Black male teacher I had ever known.

In 7th grade I received my first "C" grade from him in math. I had been part of a "desegregation bus program" designed to give folks from my part of the neighborhood a chance to attend another public elementary school just on the other side of town, which had few Black students. While at the school for grades K-6, I was taught to compete fiercely and to never accept anything less than the other (white) students. That was the lesson my mother drilled in our head and hearts. And it was gospel to me. As a result, I never achieved a grade lower than "B" and during those years was among the most popular kids in the school. I had a lot of friends who were white and my reputation as a good athlete took root during this time.

However, when it came time to choose between continuing into that feeder Junior High School or coming back to the local neighborhood school for the 3 yrs before high school, I chose the local school. It had more Black students and I missed not seeing them on a regular basis. Ironically, this decision also meant my leaving my best friend (one of the very few Black kids who lived in that area), ultimately having to compete against him when our schools met during athletic competition. Moreover, the decision also gave him access to the prettiest Black girl I had ever seen and my "girlfriend" during my early years. All of this would be his for time being though our stated pledge was to reunite at the high school and dominate all of the sports teams as a duo. Unfortunately, he would be killed by a drunk driver while riding his bike the summer prior to our reunification. It would be one of my most impactful experiences as a young person.

Coach Sessoms filled a very strong void in my life and demonstrated that Black people could wield some power. After falling one point short of a "B" in his math class, I could not contain my disappointment and my emotions ran over on the bus ride home from school. Coach somehow became aware of the intense ridicule I received from the neighborhood kids who were content with receiving average grades. He called me into his office and said, "*I am not going to give you that point but I will give you a chance to earn it ... You don't realize it but you are special. You are not an average kid and should never accept an average performance. Are you up for the challenge because if you are, I will help you*".

It was at that moment that my life changed. Not only did he have the power to change my grade (something I did not know Black folks could do), he made it clear how important high expectations are in the life of young people. Coach showed me that I could make the difference in a young person's life so long as I kept my expectations high. He asked me to rise and I did. And so I knew that if I asked others to do so, they would too.

Advice to Parents: Ten Recommendations For Parents Raising Sons Are:

1. Actively seek out and find "credible" male role models outside of the home that will either supplement or compliment any relationship your son has with his father. He has to hear how other lions roar and you have to make it happen not hope it happens.

2. Surrender some of your time with your son to these men and give them the power to positively influence and reasonably discipline your son.

3. Enroll your son in activities where STRONG and INDEPENDENT men frequent such as sports teams, academic achievement programs, and cultural activities like Rites of Passage programs. Drop him off and pick him up at the end.

4. Monitor the types of media programming (radio, television, computer, and books/magazines) that your son indulges on a regular basis. If you want him to be a strong responsible man, you HAVE to provide for him the type of programming that molds his mind in that direction. I recommend books, DVD's and other materials that focus less on money and more on athletes who were able to use

their success as a way to positively change the world. Spend less on sneakers and more on materials for learning/

5. Teach your son the value of hard work and perseverance by giving him chores. Make sure he knows that his participation in sports is connected to him taking a greater role in the upkeep of the house. Remember, hard work builds stamina, discipline, and regard for shared responsibility. Remind him that he is expected to contribute.

6. Honestly and openly discuss the reality of what it means to be a Black male in society. Share with him the lesson that simple hard work may not translate into success and that (*"fair or unfair"*) he will <u>always</u> have to out-perform his white counterpart.

7. Let it be known you <u>expect</u> him to always honor and remember his responsibility to his people and to be humble as well as graceful in both victory and defeat.

8. When he is right, let him know it through compliments and encouragement. However, when he is wrong, do NOT make up excuses or allow him to blame others (coaches, teachers, teammates, referees, etc). Accepting responsibility is the first sign of manhood.

9. Learn for yourself the <u>profound</u> differences between successful athletes like Muhammad Ali and Michael Jordan, Arthur Ashe and Tiger Woods, Mike Tyson and Jack

Johnson, Carl Lewis and Tommy Smith, John Carlos, Magic Johnson and Paul Robeson so you can teach your son how to discern the difference between a man of "his time" and a man of "all-time".

10. Make sure he understands the power of faith, spirituality, and the proper acknowledgement of a woman. She embodies these qualities and once he fully understands them, personal peace and success will follow. However failure to fully appreciate any of them will mean, life is going to be tough.

Advice to Boys: Understand that there are absolutely no short cuts in life. Young men need to accept the reality that there is a journey that they MUST take on the road to manhood and ultimately to success. Despite the new technology and seemingly wide open path to success, that the overwhelming majority of experiences they will encounter have already been encountered by those who have come before you.

Success, peace, happiness, respect, and leadership are all choices. They don't just happen just because you reach 18, 21, 25 or because your coach and peers select you. Each demands something of you and there must be a willingness on your part to actively achieve them.

Finally, you know the difference between right and wrong. Don't chase money, championships, or fame. Those are all just chapters that may or may not come on your journey of life. Remember that none of them define who you truly are. You need to have higher goals and larger aspirations.

Try to live according to your own terms but remember that how people regard you IS important so fight selfishness and ego.

"A blessing is not a blessing until you share it with someone else". So your success will ultimately be judged not in what you accomplish but how folks will regard you when you are no longer on earth.

Good luck and make the best of this life. Unfortunately, we all only get one chance to live.

Your son and Sports-Do You Have the Right Perspective?

I would definitely mandate that my son participate in sports. There are too many life lessons learned through sports and competition that cannot be duplicated via books or lectures. He will need to experience them for himself. These include individual achievement, personal success, working within a team structure, leadership, team success, and overcoming adversity. I believe that participation in sports is *the best* training ground for young men to learn these lessons at their young, impressionable ages.

The most important reason, I believe, is not so he could be popular and possibly become a star, but that he *must* submit to a higher authority if he expects to experience success. This is something he can and will have to learn and accept if he wishes to have any level of success in sports and in life. Unfortunately, too many boys see open boundaries when it comes to living their daily lives. Not enough of them have been confronted strongly enough with the reality that they cannot and will not *always* get their way. And with the two-centuries-old legacy of absent fathers in the home, an outside authority like a coach can be the difference. The coach-and-athlete relationship introduces this reality to young men in a very controlled environment. With the help of the parents, the coach-and-athlete relationship can positively reinforce the teaching of respect for both authority and elders.

Participation in sports can become a part of your son's intellectual, cultural, and personal heritage, because through sports, he can learn a unique perspective about a people (his people), who through struggle in sports found perhaps the only "true" level playing field in America. Sports can open up the doors to history, culture, politics, and revolution. Participation in sports will introduce your son to the world. He will learn geography and demographics and will be taught to navigate issues of power, wealth, business, and politics.

The goal for your son is to elevate his participation in sports, so it can connect to a larger, more global meaning. He will learn the difference between moneymakers like Michael Jordan, Allen Iverson, Charles Barkley, Michael Vick, or LeBron James and human rights icons like Arthur Ashe, Jim Brown, Bill Russell, Tommy Smith, John Carlos, Paul Robeson, and Muhammad Ali. He should be expected to follow the latter whether he is involved in sports or not. He should be encouraged through sports to positively change the world.

What are some things boys and parents need to know about the business of sports before they get in?

While my son will learn that there is a business aspect to sports, I am not going to drill him about being a "sports businessman." I think the problem with too many young men and their parents is that they are already trying to manipulate sports for business reasons without having any experience in business. When that happens, they fail. Instead of focusing on individual growth and personal achievement, they are more concerned with money and fame. *Young men need to learn to enjoy sports and stop trying to be pros.* Their parents go a long way with helping them understand that lesson.

The best and most successful athletes are first good people. They are well rounded and have a personal mission in life. They have character and integrity and are reliable and responsible. As a matter of fact, personal responsibility and accountability are keystones to their personal mantra. Their focus is *not* on money, though they have come to understand that they are in a business relationship as an athlete. However, being the best both in and out of competition is important to them, perhaps more so than their athletic accomplishments.

Boys need to understand financial gain follows general success in life and that winning is an attitude. Boys need to know that accumulating money is not the same as achieving success.

For how long does a professional athlete play?

Because boys today have access to tons of information about the careers of heroes, discouraging stories of a careers cut short due to injury will not work. Most of them will simply not believe it could ever happen to them. Therefore, I will not limit their minds as to how long their careers can be. However, the short length of an average professional career is something they should be aware of. Boys need to recognize that they will need to plan for life when their career is over. This is where personal development is so important, because through personal development comes an exploitation of one's interests for a career after sports.

A major issue for many young men participating in professional sports is that there is a chronic lack of personal development. Too many of them are just not encouraged to develop their total selves.

While most of them are taught or heavily encouraged (and of course rewarded) to learn and develop a variety of athletic talents, the development of other skills is marginalized. Therefore, unless they have great parental support or attend a well-rounded school, the large percentage of prospective professional athletes will never develop marketable skills, such as writing and speaking or learning a vocation, playing an instrument, or anything that could net them an income-earning career upon retirement from professional athletics.

A much greater emphasis on personal development and a discovery of interests is crucial for young men. As a parent, I not only need to find out what he likes or does well, but then I also will have to expose him to opportunities that will allow him to exploit his other talents.

What happens to the guys after their term is up?

Most professional athletes are never heard from in public once their playing careers are over. But because there are many prominent athletes paraded on television as highly visible sports talk-show hosts and analysts, a young boy could think that that is the future for all former pro athletes. I would teach my son that the vast majority of former professional athletes are not in the public. Most of them are working and living very regular lives and raising their families. I will inform him that those who positively exploited their time in the pros and have lived modestly are set for life. However, for those who have not been smart or who have lived beyond their means, they may find themselves having to settle for very basic work to support themselves and their families.

I would emphasize that the longer career in sports is not on the playing fields but in professions around sports, such as television, coaching, public relations, etc.

The media can be very cruel to players, and most will be assaulted negatively by the media and fans before their career is over. Some athletes are criticized so severely, they are forever scorned by the process.

What are the pros and cons of playing?

There are many benefits for participation in sports, particularly as a professional. Athletes receive great financial rewards, but their statuses as athletes afford them tremendous access to the best of everything the country has to offer. They can get into the best restaurants, the best hotels, or VIP offerings for many of the nation's (or world's) best events and activities. Life as a well-adjusted professional athlete can be incredibly fulfilling.

However, professional athletes sacrifice a tremendous amount of time and energy. The physical breakdown of their bodies and the psychological strain endured over their careers leave a significant number of athletes requiring permanent medical attention.

Many athletes have strained family relationships because their demanding travel and participation schedule makes it tremendously difficult to maintain healthy human interactions. Athletes often find themselves the target of all types of people who are interested in them only for their money or fame and not as people. Many professional athletes find themselves divorced or separated from their families, who cannot cope with the tough lifestyle and demands to remain in this industry.

Issues of who to trust and who not to trust will confuse many athletes. These are challenges that most people have to deal with but not on the level of a professional athlete. Trying to figure out who is genuinely interested in their success as a human being is something that haunts most athletes and public figures for the rest of their lives. In many instances, it can leave them bitter.

What would you tell your son if he wanted to play pro sports?

I would tell him that to pursue sports at the professional level takes a great deal of time and commitment. I would tell him that he would be expected to devote a significant amount of time and energy to sports and that he would have to make tremendous sacrifices in other, perhaps more enjoyable, activities if he wants to pursue sports at the professional level.

I would remind him of his duty to his academics, which will be the only aspect of his life that will take a higher emphasis than his sports. His failure to live up to the highest academic standards will lessen his chances of full participation in sports.

I would let him know my personal expectations about sportsmanship and his taking care of his body (drugs, alcohol, food, etc.) and discuss his commitment to not just playing the sports but training and learning about all aspects of the sports. I would discuss his friends and tell him that his peer group would need to change and that I would expect him to compete, learn, and lead.

Finally, I would remind him of a special history that African Americans have using sports to advocate for human rights and social justice. He will be expected (required) to continue that legacy if he wants my unconditional support.

Chapter 10

What I Learned and You Can Too

What I Learned (And What You Can, Too)

At the beginning of this book, I asked the following questions:

1. How do you raise successful black men?
2. Is it nature or nurture?
3. Are most successful black men academically gifted?
4. How can you change his self-perception if he can't see it?
5. How can a single mom raise a son successfully?

At the end of this book, I must say that, surprisingly, I have found some answers. Almost all of the successful men in this book had someone to guide and make sacrifices for them. Most of them also had a strong academic background. Thirteen out of the fourteen men went to college and had at least a bachelor's degree. However, the one man without the college degree is an entrepreneur and millionaire, which proves that you don't have to have a college degree to become successful. However, having a degree gives you more options and those with college degrees start making more money than those without. The entrepreneurs however were very well read, confident, and knew early in life what they wanted to do. So they worked at their own pace doing what they loved.

Another trend I noticed in most of the stories is that they gave credit to having God in their lives as guidance and/or having a strong father-figure. However at the time, many did not appreciate their father's strength when they were growing up but the fear of what the father's reaction would be if they came home with trends that were against his rules kept them in line. This was evident with Richard Jefferson, the lawyer, Chike Akua, the speaker and author, Omar Tyree, NY Times Best Selling Author and Aaron Scott, Chief Nuclear technologist. So, is it nature or nurture? It is definitely both. These men worked hard in school to develop their academic gifts and many were nurtured by family members.

The Importance of Strong Nurturing

So, men, a tip for you: be strong and decisive, but also be loving and caring. Look at the case of Omar Tyree. His stepdad came in and changed the course of his life. Yes, he was academically inclined, but without a strong father figure to discipline and guide him, there is no telling how he might have turned out. Also noted is how Omar's mother allowed the stepdad to be the dad. She did not say, "You cannot discipline my son because he is not yours." She gave him full authority, and only if she thought he was being excessive would she intervene. Dr. Sherrod spent time with his dad before he passed away, but later his scoutmaster became a surrogate dad. He was someone who believed in him, taught and guided him in the ways of manhood.

For the 70 percent of African-American households with no male figure, Mom must set the example of how a man should treat a woman. She cannot have a man in her life who disrespects and abuses her. Take note of Chris Brown, the R & B singer who abused his girlfriend Rihanna and blamed his actions on how his stepdad treated his mom. Children learn from what they live and not necessarily what you say. Multimillionaire Ephren Taylor speaks particularly to single mothers; he tells them to set the example in their own homes, but says they must find a man to be in the boy's life who can guide and support him. For the doctor, it was the scoutmaster, but for many of the others, it was their dad. So, Dad, it is crucial that you remain in your son's life as a positive role model, and if you mess up, it is never too late to change and show your son that life is about learning and making better choices. If you do not get along with the child's mother, be manly enough to put your differences aside and stay involved in your son's life. There are so many statistics that show the positive effects on a boy when his dad stays involved in his life. For this book, most of these men received nurturing into manhood, whether from a committed mother or from both parents.

What if There is Little to No Nurturing?

With seventy percent of our children growing up in homes without a father figure, It is inevitable that we will have children growing up without the proper nurturing since Mom may have to work long hours and not have enough time or energy to do the best job. However, there are men who became successful despite their surroundings just by observing behaviors in their negative environment. They have chosen to do the opposite. This is the case of Marcus Fields, the nurse and Richard Jefferson, the attorney. They grew up strong by observing a lifestyle that they did not want for themselves and chose the opposite actions.

Single Moms, your child can be your most important asset, or he can be your greatest liability. Put the time and effort into his life early. Yes, you have to work, and it's hard doing it alone, but it can be done. Anne Sherrod did it, and so did many other single moms. You have to be committed. One big mistake is expecting your son to be the man of the house. He is not a man. It gives him a false sense of manhood, and then you cannot correct his behavior because you made him the man. Treat him like your son. He should be respected, but he should not be law in your household. Use organizations like the Boy's Club, and Boy Scouts to help, but you cannot rely on an organization to raise your child. They are useful resources, but you are first and foremost. If you are not really ready to become a full-time mom, my advice is to wait before you have a child. It does not get easier once they start going to school because that is when they need you the most.

So many insecurities develop from school: Am I smart enough? Good enough? Tall enough? Too short? Too ugly? Likeable? Do I have enough friends?

At this age, his mom needs to be able to help him feel secure in his own skin. Life will be difficult for a young man once he gets to be a teenager; he needs to have all that security from childhood to sustain him. You still must set ground rules and be prepared for changes. Be assertive but supportive and loving. Most important, get a male role model in his life that he can speak to about things that men deal with, Uncles, cousins, friends, or coaches—your boy needs a male role model. Be careful about child molesters though because they are also out there. Prepare your child on how to deal with that if it ever happens. Reread the section on "The Necessary Father" by Omar Tyree.

How to Combat Negative Self Image

Changing a negative self-image is the hardest thing to do, but it can be done. First, make sure you praise your son and keep setting the bar high for him. With the slightest improvement, praise his efforts. Help him to be successful at something. This is how he will develop confidence and a positive self-image. Help him improve his academics-whether its math, writing, reading science or social studies. Sports, music, athletics, and speaking are wonderful talents to develop but not at the expense of academics. Julani Ghana was successful in sports and that was a tremendous boost to his self-esteem That confidence has sustained him and made him the man he is today. However, his parents made his academics a priority. Martin Luther King Jr, was a great orator and that helped him become one of the greatest leaders in history. But academically he was on target.

Moms and sons have a special bond. But, Moms, you can love your sons and harm them. By letting them get away with not completing their chores or not giving them enough responsibilities, you allow them to grow up lazy and they will expect things to be given to them. This does not give them self—confidence, as a matter of fact, they grow up without enough stamina to complete the tasks required for manhood. Hence so many drop out of high school and college, they are not able to stick out something that is hard and requires sacrifice. Hard work builds stamina and confidence. Most of the successful men in this book credit the hard work expected from them growing up as a foundation for the work they needed to reach their goals. A great example is that of the School Superintendent, Sam King who credits his success to the hard work his father imposed on him. Dr. Sherrod also grew up learning the value of hard work. When I spoke with his mom, Anne Sherrod, she told me she gave her son a lot of outside chores to do. He did them but would cry and complain how he did not like that kind of work. That, she said, later prepared him for the hard work of medical school because he saw how difficult life would be with manual labor if he did not have an alternate plan. Throughout all these careers, hard work and tenacity paid off.

Dads, Show Love to Your Sons

Due to the lack of male role models, too many of our boys are growing up without any idea of how a man should behave. Too many of them feel that men should be hard and not show emotion. Many times this hardness borders on becoming 'gangsta' in the way they speak, dress and conduct themselves. Dads should also teach the boys how to treat women by the way he treats the women in his life.

Yes, many African American men view hugging another man as being feminine, but there is nothing better than a good bear hug to show your son how important he is to you. Hug your son and tell him you love him and you are proud of him even though you did not receive it as a child and it may be uncomfortable for you. Your son will develop self—confidence and self—love. He will also pass on this legacy to his sons. Think of it as building a legacy for your descendants. Point out to him the importance of doing well in school, because studies show that many boys feel that reading is feminine. Dad, make sure you model reading with your son and not just watch football in order to bond. Successful men read!. Get books that reflect his culture, and tell him about what it was like for you growing up and how you made changes. Most of all, remind him of your expectations for him and what is expected in your household.

Is Education the Answer?

This is a new era. Times have changed. Years ago, you could get a job doing physical labor. Those jobs are almost non-existent. With globalization and the rise of technology, we are required to know much more earlier. Therefore, your child's academic success is first and foremost.

Do everything you can at home to develop that love of reading early. I mean from the child is an infant. Studies show that children who are read to consistently develop a love of reading. Read to your children at all times. When possible, let them read to you and explain in their own words what they have read. "Reading is fundamental" is not just a cliché but a fact. Good reading and comprehension skills lay the foundation for academic success. It is interesting to note that Hezekiah Griggs, a multimillionaire may not have gone to college, but was very literate at a young age. He and many other role models in this book were able to read and comprehend early. Dr. Michael Penn Jr., the scientist and physician, feels that reading comprehension is most crucial in getting a child ready for academic success. As an educator, I wholeheartedly agree, Currently, I teach mathematics and I have students in my fifth grade classroom who are struggling. They love math, they know their facts and are very motivated but when you test their reading skills, they are reading at a second grade level. Students are asked to solve math problems where they have to first comprehend what is asked and decide what information is necessary to solve the problem. If they are having comprehension difficulty, it affects math and all other subjects. These students, unfortunately, will always struggle in school.

Make sure your children have a quiet place to do homework and study without the distraction of TV and video games. Exposure gives your children options and builds on their experiences. So expose your children to as much positive environment as possible. Take them to the museum, library, plays, cultural events, beaches, restaurants and travel. Therefore, the thrust should be preparing the child at home. If money is tight, they can be exposed through books. There again reading comes into play. The seeds for academic success are planted at home. Books in the home and parents who read and discuss ideas, current affairs, almost always influence children to read and to care about things of the mind.

Teaching your children to make responsible choices is also important. Take Dr. Sherrod, for example; his mom gave him a choice between one expensive item of clothing or several inexpensive items that cost the same. Of course, he chose more for the money since he needed more clothes. In this case, he learned about two things: the value of money and the importance of material things in your life. So at a young age, he had to make difficult but prudent choices. This skill has helped him run a successful medical practice today.

Parents must show students that education is valued in the home from the way they speak about teachers to the insistence on completing homework assignments. But of course we know that will not happen in every home for various reasons. So this book is challenging the schools to establish a parenting initiative as well, one that encourages, teaches and supports parents to be better in order to help their children succeed.

Schools you have a responsibility as well. It is time to understand these young men that you teach and give them hope. You are not building widgets, you are building people and as such you have an awesome responsibility and you must bring humanity and dedication to this job. Show caring, understanding and a belief in their abilities. If you can't believe, then show them how they can be better and show them how much they have grown. Don't just ignore them because they are not part of your family or your race. They feel your fear and disdain and react accordingly. Do not judge them because of their skin color and gender. You are their only hope. Do not be put off by their stance of being "cool", their dress, speech and attitudes It is a coping mechanism to hide self—doubt and insecurities but it also makes them feel visible and empowered. Get to understand these boys. I recommend reading "Teaching Reading to Black Adolescent Males" by Dr. Alfred Tatum. Find out all you can about the boys you teach, their lives depend on you and how you react to them. Your job is powerful, and is not based on the money you make. You don't make things, you make people.

Our boys have a lot to deal with as African American young men. The way society views them, discrimination in schools, not having a father figure, mom not having enough time to supervise their activities and peer pressure, the deck is usually stacked against them. I was in a class for teachers who had a Masters in Educational Leadership where we were being trained on how to observe teachers. A video was shown to us of a high school teacher who was teaching a class on cells. He gave them an assignment to work in groups and then go to the other groups and explain their solution. The class was multiracial with only three African American boys sitting in the front. They clearly did not understand the task by the look on their faces. The teacher was swept away by the other students in the back of the room and never checked with this group about their understanding of the task. They finally got what they needed to do when a group of Caucasian boys came around to re-explain to them the task. How do you think this made them feel? What opinion did the other students have of them? More importantly, why were they ignored by this teacher? Did he not know that they did not understand? As a teacher, you are supposed to know all your students. So why did he not visit this group that was right underneath his nose? The answer is expectations. I believe the teacher did not expect much from them so he did not give them much of his time. This is happening in schools all across this country. This is one reason why many of our boys drop out of school.

Mental Illness

Statistics show that many of our boys in prison are suffering from mental illness. According to the Justice Department, one in three black males doing time is suffering from mental illness. The Black Mental Health Alliance for Education and Consultation, Inc invited a group of African American men to share their thoughts and experiences with regard to mental health. Their comments point to the deep rooted, systemic issues that underlie the mental health problems faced by African American men. There is a strong stigma associated with mental health problems, issues related to culture and masculinity. The scarcity of mental health providers in the black community, lack of health insurance and the few black health care professionals all add to reasons men do not seek mental health care. The following are some of the sentiments they shared with the group. "When we don't feel that we can provide for our families or protect our children, we feel worthless, depressed and we begin to turn on each other. This society only values what you do ... not who you are." "In this society, many of us feel alone, who can we turn to?" "Racism has caused many of us to feel we don't count and that our needs are not important." "Even when we do everything right and play by all the rules, we still don't get the respect we deserve, and that is very stressful. "How would you feel if you thought everyone around you was afraid of you or thought you were getting ready to do something illegal?" "Racism has caused many of us to feel that we don't count and that our needs are not important."

Stress can cause many ailments. Stress from not knowing who you really are, not knowing who you should be and worries about your future especially when you see so many people like yourself not achieving. My son would spend many hours just lying in the darkness but would not want to go see a mental health counselor. He said he was not 'crazy' he was just 'thinking' and did not need to see anyone. But depression affects the best of us. And there are many medications available to help us live productive lives. Sometimes our men have the wrong idea of what it means to be masculine. It does not mean we sit with illness and wait for it to disappear. Being a man means you realize what your human potential is and when it's out of your realm, you seek help. Maybe part of the problem is what we identify as manhood. Manhood does not mean physical toughness. Yes, you need to be mentally strong and being in great shape is always good for the mind but your physical and mental health is more important and that is where the emphasis should be.

We Have No Choice

If we don't, prepare our children for future leadership, what will happen to our race? Who will lead our communities and mentor the next generation of boys? At the core of the black male crisis is our failure to assume total responsibility for the destiny of our children—*our future*. We cannot afford to continue to live as victims. The statistics are staggering, black male unemployment is at 40% while black unemployment is at 16%. How does this affect our families? Yes, we must acknowledge the effects of racism but not dwell on it. We must use our failures to fuel the fire for our success. Too many of our boys are in jail and prison; too many of our boys don't have the right attitude about school; too many of our boys have been killed randomly by their own because they have the wrong perspective about life. In other words, we have to teach our own people the skills to succeed in today's world. According to Bill Maxwell, author of the piece in the *New York Times*, "On Campus: Grim Statistics for Our African American Men,": "Until we look inside ourselves and change our perspective on education, these grim statistics, and our men will fall further and further behind."

So as a race we cannot wait. We had to fight for freedom as a people, then we had to fight to be treated equally, we even had to fight for equal education in Roe Vs. Wade and Plessy vs, Fergusson. We won all those battles. Now we face the most important fight of all, the destruction of our people. Without our men, we cannot make it. We must fight to win the next generation of black boys so they can become the role models for generations of black men!!

Chapter 11

A Few Words for the Boys

Even if you don't have a role model, you can still be successful:
1. **Learn** from your negative surroundings. That is how many successful men did it. They knew the life they did not want to live, and they tried to avoid that life. The nurse, attorney, and engineer did it. You can too!
2. **Read**! Read! And Read!
3. **Find** someone you admire in school or church and ask if they could be your mentor. Dr. Sherrod's mentor was his coach. People will respect and admire you for taking charge of your life.
4. **Believe** in you. Do not focus on others' opinions of you. It does not count if you don't' buy' what they say about you. It is what you say to yourself every day that counts. People judge you by your actions, and your thought processes determine your actions. So what are you putting in your mind? Who are you listening to and what are they telling you? What are you reading? You are fed thousands of messages each day, make sure they are positive.

5. **Anger**—Please keep that in check. It will not help you to carry it around. It does not make you more of a man. Many times, it just gets you in trouble. Notice that *anger* is one letter short of *danger*. Find out what is hurting you and forgive. Most of all, forgive yourself.
6. **Respect**—You need to give it in order to get it. Show respect to all then you won't have a problem receiving respect. But most of all respect yourself, because when you do, you find it easier to say no to negative things in your life. *Humble Yourself.*
7. **Ego**—You need to let it go. Much of what we consider ego is false pride. You have a problem if someone disrespects you. They are usually displaying their own ignorance. You know who you are; you don't need to prove your superiority or manhood by breaking the law to teach anyone a lesson. Walk away. That is what smart, well-disciplined people do. Think about the consequences before you react, and don't hang around those people anyway. Find people who are doing positive things.
8. **Listen** twice as much as you speak, and learn from people you admire.
9. **Wait.** We live in a society where we want what we want now! In order to enjoy your life and be proud of yourself, it is important to work for what you want. Just because people are

driving expensive cars does not mean you must drive one by the time you are twenty. Build yourself first. Get your education, work, build yourself up, and save. Do not put yourself in a mountain of debt just to drive a nice car. That will come later and at a time you can afford it.

10. **Plan your life**. Do not make a decision on the spur of the moment just because you feel like it or you would get a certain status. That is the surest way of losing your money, because when you can't afford the payment and the insurance, it will surely be repossessed. Just because the car dealer worked it out so you can have the car does not mean you should. Car dealers prey on your vulnerability and will not hesitate to take that car back. Be smart. Wait! It is not just a cliché when we live by "good things come to those who wait."

11. **WATCH YOUR FRIENDS** . . . . They could be your downfall! This is called peer pressure and so many of you want to appear cool so you can be accepted. You forget about what your parents taught you because you feel you need to survive around your peers. However, thousands are in jail because they were in the wrong place at the wrong time. They were with friends when something bad happened and they had to suffer the consequences as well, even though they were not involved in the bad behavior. If you are with the people who

committed the wrong then you are also held responsible. It's called 'guilty by association'.

12. **Don't Settle for Mediocrity, be the best!**
13. **Dress for success!**

Chapter 12

Be Smart in Dealing with the Law

Too many of our boys get caught up in the system because they are not aware of their rights and the law. Make sure you are aware of all these scenarios and how you should interact with law enforcement officials. After all, ignorance is no excuse!!

Stopped Walking on the Street?

1. Officers are trying to do their job of reducing crime, so they don't usually stop you if they are not suspicious so first, stay out of trouble; if you hang out with the wrong crowd, you increase your chances of being approached by officers. Watch the people you hang out with.
2. If you are stopped, no matter how annoyed you are, approach the officer with respect, not disrespect. It is in your best interest to cooperate with the official, even if you feel you were unjustly stopped or questioned. Stay composed and conduct yourself in a mature manner. Do not try to show off around your friends, this can be detrimental.
3. Do not "bad mouth" or walk away from law enforcement

officials, even when you feel they are wrong. My son did that and was marked.

4. If they have "reasonable suspicion" that you may be carrying a weapon or illegal substance, you may be subjected to a "pat down" search. *Do not resist the search.* Obey all requests made of you unless the request poses a risk to your personal safety. In that case, ask for a meeting with the officer's supervisor... later. Please do not ask the officer.

Stopped While Driving?

1. Slow down and pull over safely when you can. If the car is unmarked and you cannot identify the driver as a uniformed police officer, drive below the speed limit to a well-lit, populated spot, then pull over.

2. Stay in the driver's seat with both hands in sight on the steering wheel. Do not exit your car unless asked to do so. (My son did not want to get out of his car because he was warned by us and so he called us.) This can be perceived as aggressive behavior and a threat to the officer's safety. Turn on your interior light if stopped at night so that they can clearly see inside.

3. Show your documents when asked but if they are in the glove compartment or under the seat, tell the officer, and then retrieve them slowly.

4. If there is "probable cause," your car can be searched without a

warrant. If you do not want your car to be searched, say, "Officer, I do not give permission for my car to be searched" in a polite manner.

5. **<u>Sign the ticket if given.</u>** Signing is not an admission of guilt, only that you received it. However, refusing to sign could result in you being arrested and facing additional charges.
6. If suspected of drunk driving, cooperate with the officers. Do not refuse breath, blood, or performance tests. If you do, it could result in loss of driving privileges and/or heavy fines.
7. Once stopped and asked for your documents, the temptation is strong to ask why you have been stopped. Resist it! Do not insist on knowing why you have been stopped first. Most officers will not provide a specific reason for the stop until they have your license and registration in hand.
8. If you wish to offer an explanation of your circumstance, do so before the officer goes to his vehicle. The officer cannot void the ticket once it's written. *If you believe you have been treated unfairly, present your case in traffic court, not to the officer along the roadside.*

If Law Enforcement Comes to Your Door (*I wish I had known this earlier, I would not have allowed officers in my home*)

1. Request to see a badge or ID card. Be pleasant but serious.
2. Make sure they are at the correct residence by asking, "How

can I help you?" They should have a warrant or be actively investigating a crime or looking for a suspect who may be in your house. If not, you can deny entry.

3. Determine the type of warrant—body or search. A body warrant means that the officers are seeking an individual and therefore cannot search drawers and places not large enough to hide a person. A search warrant allows officers all places in which the items listed on the warrant can be hidden.

You Are Arrested

1. Let them inform as to why you are being arrested. *Do not resist arrest.*
2. Call a lawyer as soon as possible. If not a lawyer, call your parent or guardian. You also have the right to privacy during the call.
3. Say nothing when being arrested, do not try to defend yourself or explain yourself to the arresting officer, because anything you say will be used against you.
4. Always keep your lawyer's number or that of the local public defender's office in your wallet or purse.

What if Law Enforcement shows Physical Abuse or disrespect?

Physical Abuse—Officer misconduct includes slaps, kicks, punches, choke-holds, beatings, flashlight and nightstick blows, tight handcuffs, and firing their weapons.

Verbal Abuse—Any name calling or use of racial slurs

The best way to avoid misconduct is to not provoke the officer while having a discussion. Showing off for friends and family will only get you arrested and possibly injured. Comply first and then seek an explanation from the officer or supervisor later.

1. Always note the name of the officers.
2. Report cases of abuse immediately following your release from police custody.
3. Record, document, and describe any case of officer misconduct, preferably in a typewritten statement.
4. Notarize your summary within three days of the incident.

It can be very intimidating to report an officer's misconduct, because we were told we had to go down to the station to file the complaint. I knew I had to accompany my son. I felt intimidated sitting there. However, if the cases are not reported, the abuse will continue. Understand that no matter what you did, police officers should always protect the citizens, not abuse them.

References

Annual Status Report on Minorities in Higher Education, American Council on Education, March 2010

"Black Men Show Five—fold Increase in Prison Rates", New York Times, November 20, 2008

Bonzcar, Thomas P., US Department of Justice, Bureau of Justice Statistics, "Prevalence of Imprisonment in the US Population, 1974-2001"

Durose, Matthew R., and Langan, Patrick A, Bureau of Justice Statistics, State Court Sentencing of Convicted Felons, 1998 : Statistical Tables (Washington DC:US Department of Justice, December, 2001) Table 25

Fellner, Jamie and Mauer, Marc, "Losing the Vote: The Impact of Felony Disenfranchisement Laws in the United states" (Washington DC: Human Rights watch & The Sentencing Project, 1998) p.8

Key Recommendations from Punishment and Prejudice: racial Disparities in the war on Drugs (Washington DC: Human Rights watch, June 2000)

Kunjufu, Jawanza. Countering the Conspiracy to Destroy Black Boys. Volume III, Chicago, IL 1990.

Mauer, M. & Huling, T., Young Black Americans and the Criminal Justice System: Five Years later (Washington DC: The sentencing Project, 1995)

Maxwell, Bill. On Campus: Grim Statistics for African American Men

Sabot, William J,. PhD, Couture, Heather, Bureau of Justice Statistics, Prison inmates at midyear 2007 (Washington DC: US department of Justice, June 2008)

Substance Abuse and Mental Health Services Administration, National Household Survey on Drug Abuse: Summary Report1998 (Rockville, MD: Substance abuse and Mental health Services Administration, 1999) p.13

Tatum, Alfred. Teaching Reading to Black Adolescent Males. Portland, Maine: Stenhouse Publishers, 2005.

The Schlott Fifty State Report on Black Males and Education. www.Blackboysreport.org.2011

Welch, Ronald H. and Angulo, Carlos T., Justice on Trial: Racial Disparities in the American Criminal Justice System (Washington,

DC: Leadership Conference on Civil Rights/Leadership Conference Education Fund, May 2000)

Wynn, Mychal. Empowering African American Males. Georgia, Rising Sun Publisher. 2005. Print

Made in the USA
Columbia, SC
17 March 2019